POTTERY BARN

bathrooms

TEXT
judith nasatir

PHOTOGRAPHY
hotze eisma

STYLING
anthony albertus

EXECUTIVE EDITOR
clay ide

Oxmoor House®

Oxmoor House.

Oxmoor House books are distributed by Sunset Books
80 Willow Road, Menlo Park, CA 94025

Oxmoor House and Sunset Books are divisions of
Southern Progress Corporation

SUNSET BOOKS

Vice President, General Manager Rich Smeby
Vice President, Editorial Director Bob Doyle
National Account Manager Brad Moses

POTTERY BARN

President Laura Alber
Senior Vice President, Design & Product Development Celia Tejada
Vice President, Creative Services Clay Ide
Editor Samantha Moss
Photo Coordinator, Special Projects Gina Risso

WELDON OWEN

Chief Executive Officer John Owen
President Terry Newell
Chief Operating Officer Larry Partington
Vice President, International Sales Stuart Laurence

Creative Director Gaye Allen
Vice President, Publisher Roger Shaw
Business Manager Richard Van Oosterhout

Associate Publisher Shawna Mullen
Art Director Joseph De Leo
Managing Editor Peter Cieply
Production Director Chris Hemesath
Color Manager Teri Bell
Photo Coordinator Elizabeth Lazich

Pottery Barn Bathrooms was conceived and produced by
Weldon Owen Inc.
814 Montgomery Street, San Francisco, CA 94133
in collaboration with Pottery Barn
3250 Van Ness Avenue, San Francisco, CA 94109

Set in Simoncini Garamond™ and Formata™

Color separations by AGT–Seattle
Printed in Singapore by Tien Wah Press (Pte.) Ltd.

First printed 2003
10 9 8 7 6 5 4

Library of Congress Control Number 2003106156
ISBN 0-8487-2761-4

The Ultimate Retreat

The bathroom is the ultimate retreat, the space where, even in a busy home, we can find the peace and privacy to indulge in a candlelit soak, or to enjoy an hour of spa-inspired treatments. As the room where we bathe and refresh, it must always be practical and functional. But like any area of your home, it's the personal details that make it truly comfortable. Furnished with style, a bathing space can be sumptuous and unique.

At Pottery Barn, we're devoted to the idea that your home can be an endless source of inspiration. We believe that decorating with style should be easy and fun, and a large part of our mission is to demystify interior decorating. We design our furnishings to work in many different spaces, and we fill our catalogs with inventive, achievable ideas. This book is full of inspiration and tips we've gleaned from decorating more than five thousand rooms during the past ten years. We shoot all our photography in real homes, often in one day, so our ideas must always be accessible and easy to accomplish. What we've learned over the years is that any room, anywhere, offers unique creative opportunities. We believe your home should be an expression of you, your family, and your lifestyle. In *Pottery Barn Bathrooms*, you'll see how easy it can be to create luxurious, comfortable bathing spaces with an appealing style all your own.

THE POTTERY BARN DESIGN TEAM

contents

your style

There's often a divide between the bath of your dreams and the reality of your own bathroom, but it doesn't have to stay that way. With a little imagination and a few creative basics, you can achieve a new look more easily than you might think. More than a century ago, Louis Sullivan, the great American architect, said, "Form follows function." In the bath, nothing could be more true. In almost every feature of the space, the forms (vessels, pipes, fixtures, and fittings) were created specifically to serve their mechanical purpose. The first step in get-

Choose patterns carefully, because they can be emphasized in the smaller space of the bathroom. Think in terms of wet and dry when selecting textures, and take into account how they'll react to the wet environment of the bathroom.

The layout of the bathroom is defined by the fixtures: tub, shower, sink, toilet, and built-in storage. Although not impossible to replace, these are the more challenging items to change. New colors or a fresh crop of textures, however, can also alter the feeling of the space. Bringing in some furniture – a simple upholstered chair or a

In design, there is never one right way, there's only the way that's right for you. Finding it isn't hard. Just trust your tastes and follow your instincts.

ting the bath of your dreams is learning to understand those forms and the materials they come in, then finding the best ways to work with them to create a comfortable and satisfying bath.

A bathroom's style usually evolves over time. Often, we only begin to realize whether a space works – if it suits its users, if it's comfortable, if it pleases all the senses – after we've lived with it for a while. Follow the lead of design professionals who create rooms for a living, and begin your project by gathering a collection of style ideas that appeal to you – from books, magazines, even inspirations from nature. Look at swatches of new colors in the real light of your bathroom.

low bench – adds comfort. A quick change to the quality of the room's light, accomplished through new window treatments, mirrors, bulbs, or the light fixtures themselves, can completely transform the atmosphere of the bathroom.

Be creative in your choices of the little things, and keep in mind that it doesn't take much to make a dramatic change in the bath. From the smallest powder room to the largest suite, every space offers individual opportunities for style. Styling a bath is as much a process of planning as of decorating. The fact that your space may be limited can work to your advantage: it means that even the smallest details will go a long way.

A Simply Perfect Bathroom

Simple pleasures are often the most satisfying, especially in the bath: the clean sweep of white wainscoting, well-placed windows, the perfect shade of periwinkle blue illustrate the axiom "less is more." This uncomplicated bathroom easily integrates fixtures, finishes, and accents with style.

There are probably as many ideas of what constitutes a well-styled bathroom as there are people who use them. How to discover which is right for you? Start with the basics. The size and shape of each space often suggests a particular style of decor. If you treat the room simply, starting with clean finishes, lots of white, and pleasing accents, you can build from there and add accessories to the room over time.

The secret to the classic, integrated bath shown here is the easy way it combines function (all the elements needed for grooming and cleanliness) and ornament (the little extras). If you look closely, you'll notice that every working element of this bath (the tub, the sink, the shower, and the fittings) is also a decorative asset. The attractive features of this design, its openness and light touch, result from such practical considerations as a generous tub, beautifully finished faucets, well-placed mirrors, and easy-to-clean finishes. In the bathroom, these few carefully planned elements create a design whole that is greater than the sum of its parts.

Mirrored shadow boxes, *left*, create additional "windows" and convenient, but barely protruding, display and storage ledges. Sachets filled with dried lavender dangle from the side hooks and scent the room. **A claw-foot tub**, *right*, with nickeled feet sports a faucet with a handheld shower, in keeping with its vintage style.

Simple doesn't necessarily mean spare. In this bath, every function has its own area. Here, walls and doors define distinct spaces for showering, bathing, grooming, and so on. Separating functions into individual areas in this way is a clever visual strategy that also helps the users. The enclosed shower and screened toilet not only leave the main room open and uncluttered, but also allow more than one person at a time to use the space.

The clean finishes, the period details, and the profiles of the moulding integrate the room's decor. An antique-style, extra-long tub with nickeled feet sets the tone for materials and decorative details. The vintage look extends to the hexagonal floor tiles and black tile accents, a scheme common in baths of the early twentieth century. Faucets are also reproductions of period pieces. Extra-long towel bars and a tempered-glass shower door are contemporary touches that bring the room's style up to date.

A pocket door, *left*, screens the toilet and is in keeping with the traditional look of the room's painted wood wainscoting. **An apothecary bottle**, *right*, on a tubside chest holds a sprig of fresh lavender; these attractive bottles bring clear color to the decor and are great for decanting bath oils.

A place for everything, and a few well-placed details, help make a bathroom feel open though not austere. Beautiful materials make simple elements shine; sculptural forms need no other ornament.

A reproduction vintage pedestal sink adds minimal bulk to a narrow setting; angular lines echo the moulding. The medicine cabinet is inset, so it doesn't interrupt the flow of space. The corridor leading from the wet space to the screened toilet area includes a walk-in closet.

Design Details

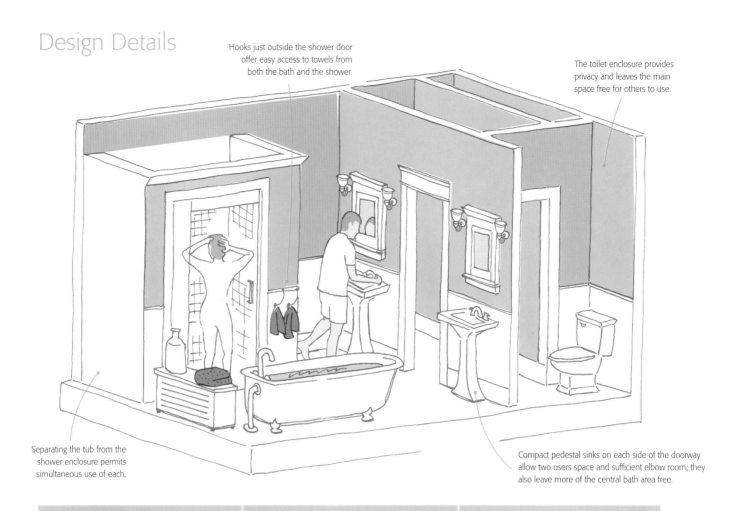

Hooks just outside the shower door offer easy access to towels from both the bath and the shower.

The toilet enclosure provides privacy and leaves the main space free for others to use.

Separating the tub from the shower enclosure permits simultaneous use of each.

Compact pedestal sinks on each side of the doorway allow two users space and sufficient elbow room; they also leave more of the central bath area free.

Color Palette

There may be no combination more classic, or more pleasing, than blue and white in the bath. Blue is the color of sky and water, and a primary color long associated with peace and tranquility. Broad expanses of white make tight spaces seem larger, while white trim defines architectural elements clearly against the walls. Bath towels in bright, clear lilac complement the cool color palette.

Room Plan

Separating the bathroom's functional areas allows more than one person to use the space at a time. Painting the wainscoting, mouldings, and door frames white neatly integrates the room with its fixtures. Over-sink medicine cabinets are recessed and flush with the wall. This modern bathroom gets its traditional look from vintage-style elements, including a footed tub, wainscoting, hexagonal floor tiles, and plaster walls. (Plaster was the construction material of choice for coating interior surfaces until the 1940s.)

Materials

Wainscoting The wood paneling on the lower part of this bathroom's walls is traditional tongue-and-groove wainscoting.

Hexagonal tile Multisided ceramic tiles, often white with black accents, were commonly used on bath floors around the turn of the last century.

Plaster This durable, sound-absorbent wall material can be easily painted, stenciled, or wallpapered.

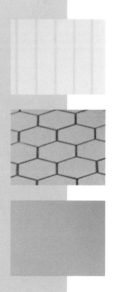

Fresh from Nature

An outdoor shower is a vacation-home luxury that conjures the spirit of summer. A sunny view, teak flooring, and an awning-striped curtain are all you need for instant cabana style.

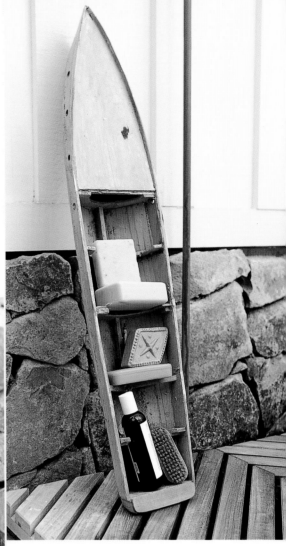

An open-air shower on a patio is a good place to wash off sand and salt, and a perfect way to make the most of natural surroundings. A platform of water-resistant teak flooring, a ledge made of stone, and galvanized accessory containers are all designed to weather beautifully through showers and rainfall.

Galvanized and enameled graniteware buckets, *left*, are novel vehicles for shower supplies. **A miniature skiff,** *above*, holds soaps and bath scrubs. **Teak garden tiles,** *right*, offer traction and adequate drainage.

space

Space is defined both by a room's physical boundaries and by the atmosphere within them. In a bathroom, permanent fixtures are the building blocks of the room: the sink, toilet, tub, and shower. Their placement, and therefore the primary orientation of the space, depends on what can't be seen: the plumbing lines. When designing a bathroom, start with the givens of fixtures, then determine the rest.

Take stock of what you've got. Consider square footage. Can you expand? Where should storage go? Look for ways to create zones within the to arranging it. Square rooms draw attention to the center of their space. Oblong rooms are flexible and easy to divide into zones. A curved wall provides an element of theatricality, as well as a sense of cocooning embrace.

The impression of space is also affected by the proportions of the room. A corridor-like bathroom may feel crowded at first, but its long walls can be lined with shelves to lift storage off the ground, giving you more usable floor space and making the room feel taller and wider. Low ceilings encourage fixtures with a compact profile.

The way you shape and style your bathroom's space determines not only how it will function, but how it will feel. Pay attention to the details.

room, and try to organize areas by activities. If you have a generous expanse of open space, for example, consider installing a deep tub for relaxing soaks and a separate stall for quick showers. If you can't change the fixtures, you can change a space with furniture. Large spaces feel cozier and more comfortable when they include an upholstered chair for curling up and relaxing.

Whatever size your space, consider subdividing areas with screens or partitions. Screening a large bath creates intimacy; separating the toilet from the sink can make a small bath more efficient. The shape of your bathroom profoundly affects how you feel in it and the best approach

Many of us have to work with limited space in the bathroom, so creativity is most needed here. Small rooms don't have to be less accommodating; on the contrary, they can be embellished with lavish materials or luxurious accessories.

Other things will affect the nature of your space as well: the slope of ceilings, the quality and quantity of light, the number and location of windows, and the palette of materials. Space is affected, too, by the temperature (warm or cool) and amount of color, the use of pattern on walls or floors, and the placement of furnishings and display elements. Design is, after all, in the details. The art is in relating them to each other.

A Family-Friendly Bath

Designed to host users great and small, this bathroom combines the informality of a vacation home with the practicality of a hardworking bath. Relaxed style allows lounging or bathing; storage at all levels and thoughtful personal touches create a customized space for each user.

Imagine a bath that not only allows room for bathing and grooming, but also welcomes reading, dozing, and congregating as well. If you're fortunate enough to have the luxury of space, consider the option of a multi-use bath designed for the whole family.

This unique bathroom is a good example. A generous central bath is the focus of the room, but it's surrounded by all the comforts of a family living space: upholstered furniture, displays of personal photos, toys, reading material – nearly everything a family that shares a busy bathing space together could want.

When you're planning a bath for multiple uses, organization is paramount. Consider all the possible activities you may want to pursue (bathing, reading, playing), and what each requires in terms of floor space, furnishings, and materials. Managing clutter is always critical, but even more so when spaces are shared. If you make the most of under-sink storage with modular units or open shelves, as is done here, you'll ensure that everything has a place. You'll also keep floor space clear for other uses.

A toy truck, *left*, used as a soap holder adds a note of whimsy.
Simple pine-plank shelves, *right*, create plenty of storage and provide surface space for displaying family items. In this family bathroom, surfaces and materials are suited to children and their needs. The shelves and the stained and sealed plywood floor are easy to clean and water resistant.

Your bathing space can be as big as your imagination. Bring in comfortable furnishings and personal accents, and provide plenty of storage for all.

Bath time takes on a whole new meaning in such a comfortable space. Light wood finishes and a warm color palette create a cheerful, vibrant atmosphere, inviting users to linger. Moveable storage options allow adults to transform the room easily from a busy, kid-cleaning staging area into a grown-up relaxing zone.

A deck-mounted tub, *left*, is reached by wide, easy steps, which also keep toys and essentials handy. The basic pine-plank construction is an inexpensive solution for a vacation home. Side-by-side sinks have rounded corners and easy-to-manipulate faucets. Multiple sinks mounted along a continuous counter ensure that there's plenty of room for everyone. **Orchid baskets hung on pulleys**, *above*, store bath accessories and toys. Their moisture resistance makes them ideal in the bath.

This tall, standing chalkboard is a drawing slate for young children and a place for adults' lists. Several seating areas around the bathtub, including the tubside steps and a comfy chair with a washable slipcover, can be used to oversee kids or just for long-term lounging.

Design Details

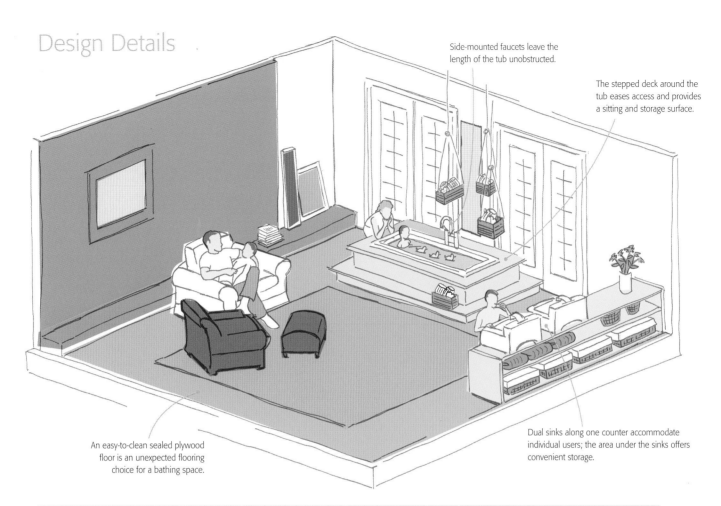

Side-mounted faucets leave the length of the tub unobstructed.

The stepped deck around the tub eases access and provides a sitting and storage surface.

An easy-to-clean sealed plywood floor is an unexpected flooring choice for a bathing space.

Dual sinks along one counter accommodate individual users; the area under the sinks offers convenient storage.

Color Palette

A red focal wall and red accessories warm up an otherwise neutral palette of white and brown. Pairs of French doors and white on all but the focal wall make the room feel airy and open. Natural surface materials such as leather upholstery and wood floors and shelves suit a casual bath that's shared by a whole family. The warm color palette is cheerful for children and pleasing to adults.

Room Plan

Setting the bathtub on a platform turns the room's key element into its central focus. The seating group angles toward the tub for easy conversation. Deck-mounting the tub in a stepped pine platform creates ease of access and also provides sitting space. Mounting the faucets on the side leaves the tub unobstructed. Storage is everything in a multipurpose bath: deep pine shelves with wicker baskets line the long walls, and under-sink areas store bath toys and toiletries. Two sets of French doors provide both light and ventilation.

Materials

Pine The knottier the pine, the more rustic a room feels. Here, casual pine-plank shelves and a tub deck join with a sealed plywood floor.

Wicker Woven from flexible twigs or branches, often from the willow tree, wicker makes durable storage baskets and hampers.

Porcelain This nonporous ceramic – the classic material for bathtubs, sinks, and toilets – is durable and easy to clean.

Zoning a Wet and Dry Room

Make a bathing space more functional and relaxing by dividing it into different zones. Thoughtful space planning can help you create areas that encourage the pursuit of leisure – enjoying the morning paper and a cup of coffee – alongside areas for bathing, grooming, and dressing.

What makes the ideal bathing space? There's never just one perfect approach, but subdividing a bathroom into wet and dry areas comes close. Take cues from spa planning, where whole rooms are dedicated to soaking and steaming or rejuvenating and resting. Wet/dry bath layouts subdivide the room into discrete zones for washing, grooming, and relaxing. To do this most successfully, you need a generous space that's large enough to accommodate seating, storage, and anything else you might want to keep out of the range of splashes from the sink or tub. You can create zones within one room, or, if you're planning to expand, you can add an area like a sunroom and use different flooring to mark the zone change and visibly delineate the space.

Bath design doesn't have to adhere to any typical notion of a cool, clean, tiled chamber. The room shown here is rustic and cottage-like, with its wall structure exposed. It is painted in a neutral palette of pure white offset with blue-gray, and each zone is fitted out with a polished fixture. The overall effect is that of a comfortably furnished space where one also happens to bathe.

A small table, *left*, for towels and accessories establishes a dry spot between the sink and the tub, providing a useful bridge between two wet zones. **A generous bathtub**, *right*, like this Empire-style tub, inspired by Roman baths and traditional European tubs, invites long, luxurious soaks.

The primary concern that governs the placement of furnishings in a bathroom is distance from the water sources. Even when you do keep furniture at a safe distance, the atmosphere is humid throughout the room. Because of this, ventilation and sunlight are key features to plan into your space. This room benefits from windows on three sides that provide air circulation and plenty of sunlight. A high ceiling fan or a directional vent are other good options.

Rugs on a painted plywood floor, *left,* subtly mark zones: a terry mat is layered over a crushed bamboo one at the tub; a plush rug defines a sitting area. A quilt rack keeps towels at hand.
A cotton-slipcovered chair, *above and left,* offers comfort; a bureau adds storage and display space.

Separate the dry zone visually by furnishing it as completely as possible, but keep materials in mind. Use furniture that is sealed or painted to resist water. Wood floors, especially, should be treated with several coats of urethane. A general rule on maintenance: when water stops beading on any surface, it's time to give it a new protective coating.

Slipcovers help to protect upholstered pieces from dampness and are easy to keep clean. A number of fabrics fare well in the bathroom. Natural linens have a sheen that helps to deflect moisture. Cotton twills and denims wash well and soften over time. Terry cloth makes an easy leap from towels to upholstery fabric. Chenille has a soft texture that resembles terry cloth and velour, though it's less absorbent. For the floor, mats made of reeds and grasses hold up nicely and in some cases release a sweet scent when humidity is high.

Wide-valve fixtures, *left*, fill deep tubs quickly; this tub-filler faucet and handheld shower are reproductions of English bath fittings. A billowy curtain is adorned with sparkling teardrop crystal beads. **Plants in the bathroom**, *right*, add color and scent to a serene white space. Sedum and echevaria plants live in stone-filled lanterns that suggest these succulents' own native dry zones.

Displaying original artwork in the bath can be a risky proposition. Baths with ample ventilation allow art to be displayed, as long as it is placed out of the splash zone of fixtures. A series of paintings (abstracts inspired by the sea and desert) adorn these walls, playing off the room's wet/dry theme.

Design Details

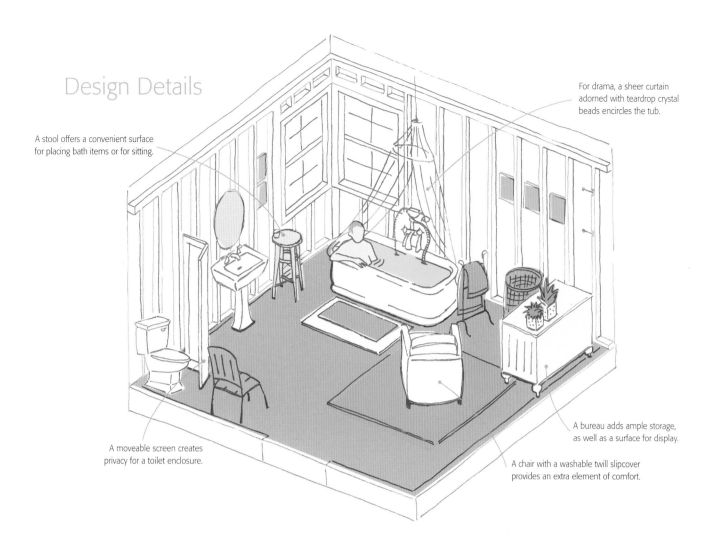

A stool offers a convenient surface for placing bath items or for sitting.

For drama, a sheer curtain adorned with teardrop crystal beads encircles the tub.

A moveable screen creates privacy for a toilet enclosure.

A bureau adds ample storage, as well as a surface for display.

A chair with a washable twill slipcover provides an extra element of comfort.

Color Palette

A palette can energize a space or calm it down. Choosing pale colors with little difference in value, like this palette of white, blue-gray, and taupe, creates a peaceful space that becomes even dreamier in the late afternoon light. Accessories, such as the sky- and seascape paintings, introduce subtle variations on the color theme. Cooler and more muted than pastel blues, the grayed blues have a minimalist, tranquil quality.

Room Plan

In a large bath, it makes sense to plan for wet and dry activities and to configure elements that bridge the two, such as putting a towel rack between the tub and dressing area. Area rugs can help with zoning, too. Use luxurious fabrics in the dry zone as counterpoints to water-friendly materials near the tub. Every room can always use more storage, so look for furniture in moisture-resistant finishes that can be used to store bath items. Don't forget hooks, which create storage out of thin air. If you have enough room, bring in a bureau or chest.

Materials

Painted wood Painting the wood floors and walls produces easy-to-clean surfaces that complement the bright, white space.

Bamboo Made from hollow-stemmed woody grasses, crushed bamboo rugs add natural texture.

Twill Usually cotton, this strong textile is woven to create diagonal ridges across its surface for durability, making it a good choice for slipcovers. Denim is a twill.

How to Make the Most of Space

A few simple changes can increase available space, or the perception of it, in the bathroom. Using clear materials, choosing a light color scheme, and employing scaled-down fixtures are just some of the design tricks that make even the smallest bath feel more open and airy. Mirrors are another decorative element that can enhance a sense of spaciousness. Mounting sinks on the walls saves precious inches, and the absence of pedestals and vanities gives the illusion of increased floor area. Hanging shelves above eye level, so they're not immediately visible when entering the bath, also opens up visual space.

A clear view, *left*, and see-through materials can make a bath appear larger. If views and privacy afford the indulgence, consider framing your shower stall on three sides with glass. For a similar effect, try glass shower doors, or use see-through or mostly see-through shower curtains, or any other screening elements (such as fabrics) that delineate areas without completely blocking light. Even just a few transparent accessories can create the perception that a space is more expansive than it is. **Louvered screens**, *above*, are one of the many ways to carve out dedicated zones within a large bath. Easy to install and flexible, screens establish intimate areas that surround the body and block any drafts or breezes. Partial-height walls serve the same function, creating subsidiary spaces within the open expanse of the room.

Fixtures designed for children, *left*, especially low-height sinks, allow kids to have dedicated space of their own within a family bath. Storage is always a critical element in freeing up space. Installing baskets on pulleys for stowing tub toys or hanging easy-to-reach hooks for shoes and clothes helps keep the floor safely uncluttered. A small chair offers seating for young bathers and holds towels or a robe.

Separating the sink from the toilet, *above*, creates two private areas within a single bathroom space and allows more than one person at a time to use the room.

fixtures

The bathroom revolves around key fixed elements. The fixtures – the sink, tub, toilet, and shower – are almost always givens. So unless you're building from scratch, you probably have less flexibility in designing (or transforming) your bath than you might wish. The physical constraints involved in controlling the flow of water are, after all, what this space is really about. Fixtures are by definition immovable; their positions depend upon access to the water supply. And these features almost always remain the same from bath to bath. This doesn't mixes, and directs the water flow. Fittings, like fixtures, come in countless shapes and styles, often with several mounting options for tubs, showers, and sinks. They are often made of a combination of materials, from metals to semi-precious stones, porcelain, and glass. Their range will inspire you to dress your bathroom up or down, according to your own style.

Experiment with the little things. Complements are always welcome, especially when it comes to details. Search for towel bars, drawer pulls, paper holders, medicine cabinets, and

Selecting the fixtures and fittings is one of the pleasures of planning a bathroom. Fittings are the room's jewelry, and show your style and flair.

mean you can't be creative. Use your imagination. Fixtures are vessels, and like containers of any kind, they come in a variety of materials, shapes, styles, sizes, colors, and finishes. You may like newly minted designs or reproductions of older ones; you might prefer salvaged and reconditioned antique pieces. Or, you may have found an everyday object, meant for another use, that you love and that you're able to adapt creatively and use in place of a standard fixture.

Even if you're not installing new fixtures, you can still accessorize. The fittings – the taps and spouts, the faucetry – are the jewelry of the bathroom, the decorative hardware that controls, mirrors that add personality. Even the smallest, simplest bathrooms can be wonderfully clever. Put a rack on the wall for jewelry so you can try on different pieces as you dress in the morning; find a small antique curtain rod and mount it on the wall for use as a towel bar; replace a plain medicine cabinet mirror with an adjustable, floating one, or attach an antique frame to the existing mirror to give it a new look.

Humor, creativity, and a flash of the unexpected can transform an everyday space. In any bath, there's always room for invention. Small details count as much as large ones in a space where you use every element every day.

Fitting Out a Wet Room

By definition, every bath is a wet room, at least in part. A current trend in bath design takes that idea to the limit. A true "wet room" removes all the usual barriers between wet areas and dry to create an open-plan bath that's multifunctional, free-form, and a pure physical delight.

There's a delicate balance between practicality and pleasure, and it's different for everyone. Some people love the sensuality and easy maintenance of an outdoor shower. Others like the feel of open space but nevertheless require a sense of privacy for true personal comfort. Still others happily settle into the luxury of a good long soak. If you desire all of the above, you might find that a wet room suits you. More and more homeowners are rethinking the traditional boundaries of the bathroom and opening themselves up to the freedom of a wet room.

A wet room commonly incorporates several, if not all, of the expected fixtures (shower, bathtub, sink) without ordinary space dividers (shower enclosure, shower curtain). A completely open plan demands generous floor and wall space. Proper distance between water sources ensures that common bath accoutrements like towels stay dry, whether hung, set on surfaces, or folded into containers. You'll find that some of these suggestions for dealing with zoning in a wet room also may be useful in small bathrooms.

A mix of matte and polished finishes, *left*, clear and frosted materials, and rough and smooth surfaces delight both the hand and the eye. The tub platform and floor are clad in slate tiles, a suitable type of stone for bath flooring because its irregular surface disperses water and provides some traction underfoot. **Water-smoothed river rocks**, *right*, along with abalone shells and starfish, are naturally beautiful decorations in this shower area.

A wet room knows no boundaries. Water runs freely, and bathing becomes a more sensual experience. Surfaces are best chosen for their natural appearance and their ability to resist water.

Good ventilation is critical in a wet bath. The more air you can circulate through this space, the better. An ideal wet room might feature multiple windows as well as direct access to the outdoors. The bathroom shown here has French doors that open outside to a porch, so users can pass straight into the shower area from the exterior without tracking dirt through the house.

A wet room's free-flowing space can be both extremely sensible and exceptionally luxurious, depending on your selection of fixtures, fittings, and finishes. Practicality suggests sticking with matte finishes, which tend not to show water spots, for the broad expanses of walls and floor. To add visual interest, counter the matte surfaces with plenty of high-gloss accents: porcelain fixtures, chrome hardware, and glass, acrylic, or polished metal accessories.

A deep tub, *left*, resting on a slate-paved pedestal, dominates the space and makes the most of spectacular views. Floor-mounted faucetry leaves the tub's full length unobstructed for bathing. On the windows, textured acrylic panels filter sunlight. **Bath accessories**, *above and left*, live in stainless-steel mesh baskets that drain easily and in acrylic jars underneath the sink.

A French-style chrome faucet is elevated and easy to clean. Above the sink, mirrored panels are built into the center row of windows. An antique soap holder is attached to the sill beside the sink.

Design Details

Placing the shower in the corner provides the user with a pair of embracing walls.

Window panels flank a center strip of mirrors over the sink, offering utility, light, and views.

A long, deep tub set on a slate platform elevates the bather to window level.

The floor slopes slightly to the drain, taking advantage of gravity.

Slate tiles' natural texture provides more traction when wet than highly polished or honed stone surfaces.

Color Palette

A simple color plan in a mix of matte and polished finishes allows this sophisticated space to assert its geometry. For a similar effect, choose one color for vertical surfaces, and another, whether dark or light, for the floor. In this bath, the walls are painted in a soft, golden wash of color, and the floor is a flinty, slate-green that gets darker when wet. White fixtures stand out against this simple backdrop.

Room Plan

Getting rid of interior barriers like shower curtains and enclosures opens a bath up completely, making it a true "wet room." This approach requires generous floor space to keep adequate distance between water sources and bath items that you want to keep dry. Putting the shower in the corner suggests a sense of enclosure. A wire basket next to the tub keeps bath necessities within easy reach and drains easily. Hooks and clear acrylic containers with lids help keep bath accessories organized, in sight, and dry.

Materials

Slate A natural stone that comes in a range of colors, this attractive, water-resistant material for tub platforms and floors disperses water slicks, helping with traction.

Textured acrylic This synthetic material is light-weight and easy to wash. In this bath, textured acrylic window panels filter sunlight.

River rock Stones in a range of colors and patterns, polished smooth by a river's flow, offer natural beauty.

Creating an Outdoor Oasis

An outdoor bath is one of life's finer pleasures. You can be creative with the fixtures you choose and how you install them. Indulge your imagination and create an open-air room with exposed plumbing and out-of-the-ordinary fixtures made from everyday objects.

An outdoor bathing space can be so much more than just a shower set up for a quick rinse. Traditionally, an outdoor bath has been just a spigot tapped into existing pipes for economy. Today's sophisticated versions incorporate custom fixtures with sleek fittings. Reconsider the basic stall of metal or wood. You can use indoor goods – from linen curtains to mirrors – to outdoor advantage.

Suppose, for example, that you want to construct a completely open-air room, one with both tub and shower. You could use conventional fixtures and faucetry, but an exterior setting presents a fine opportunity to try something unusual and more in tune with a garden location. In this outdoor bath, a galvanized metal bin has been converted to a bathtub and equipped with gleaming chrome fittings: a drenching "rain" showerhead and a mixed-channel tub filler – a format that delivers hot and cold water through a single spout. The plumbing is designed to be on display (rather than concealed behind a wall), with finely finished and polished parts and ceramic lever handles.

As refreshing as an afternoon cloudburst, *left*, a drenching showerhead is ideally suited to the outdoor bath. It offers a wider area of spray than conventional showerheads and is mounted overhead rather than in front of the bather. **Tubs come in all shapes and sizes**, *right*. This galvanized bin, from a feed and farm supply outlet, was plumbed for drainage to create a functional tub for enjoying an outdoor soak.

If you want to explore unusual fixtures, think function first, and look for precedents. It helps to understand what different forms are made for, how the choice of materials might affect them, and what the environment requires. A tub, after all, is essentially just a large waterproof vessel. What else could serve the same purpose? If you use metal, is it galvanized or otherwise rustproof? Copper, for example, commonly used for tubs in the nineteenth century, is a great conductor of heat but corrodes unless it is sealed or lined with tin. There are no absolutes. An outdoor bath is always custom-designed, so take advantage of the setting and find fixtures and fittings that work for you.

This open-air bath, *left*, reveals a highly personal approach to design. All the necessary fixtures are present, but in unexpected forms: potted flowers stand in for walls, a wood chair holds bath supplies, and a mirror and hooks turn the side of a shed into a vanity area. **A galvanized metal box**, *above*, stores fresh towels, keeping them clean and tidy.

Installing fixtures outdoors transforms the everyday bathing experience, so don't feel compelled to choose ordinary ones. Most indoor showers have concealed plumbing: valves and water-delivery pipes are behind a wall, and only the showerhead and valve trims are visible. For an outdoor shower, consider an open system highlighted by a polished metal finish.

This wooden tray, *left*, used for bath accessories, is actually a vintage carpenter's tool caddy. **A cluster of camp lanterns**, *above*, dangles by the tub, shedding warm light for nighttime bathing. White tie-top curtains and a screen of plants provide a measure of privacy.

Color Palette

You needn't go far to incorporate the colors of nature into an outdoor bath; they're there waiting for you. Here, the faded paint colors of the background walls, especially the almost Tuscan pink, add soft, earthy notes. For hot climates and summer homes, white and blue is a classic combination. A white linen shower curtain picks up the white of the flowers; blue towels mirror the blue of the sky. Blue also is a color that fades well when exposed to the elements. Fresh green in a range of hues rounds out this outdoor plant-filled palette.

Materials

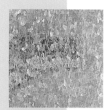

Galvanized metal Adding a thin metallic layer, often zinc, over another metal to prevent corrosion produces galvanized metal. This outdoor tub shows its distinctive mottled finish. Other options for outdoor tubs include porcelain and acrylic.

Weathered wood Wood ages in a variety of ways. Some woods, like cedar, turn a silvery gray with exposure to the elements. Painted wood can fade and peel. Pressure washing or sandblasting can simulate the patina of age without the wait.

Linen Linen is woven of yarns that are spun from the durable fibers of the flax plant. It is twice as strong as cotton, yet softens with washing. An ideal summer-weight fabric, lightweight linen provides a curtain of privacy, while still allowing sunlight to shine through.

Tub and Shower Basics

Tubs and showers are virtually rooms unto themselves, and they needn't be rooms just for one. But "room" goes to the heart of the matter when you're considering bathing spaces. It is essential, and possible, to fit comfortably in the place where you bathe. Tubs, like sinks, come in a myriad of shapes and offer many installation options. They can be anywhere in a space – aligned with a wall, skirted (enclosed with molded panels), or tucked into decks that can be clad in the materials of your room. Whatever installation you choose, try the tub out first: there's no better way to ensure the performance of your bathtub than sitting in it.

When selecting a tub, be sure that you can submerge comfortably, with your shoulders well under the rim and legs extended. Sizes have increased greatly from vintage and mid-century designs. Today the standard is 5½ feet by 32 inches, but you can find stock sizes much larger – all the way up to 6 feet 6 inches by 39 inches for a double-occupancy oval. Regular depths measure between 14 and 16 inches; at 20 to 21 inches, luxurious soaking tubs are even deeper. How you plan to use the tub – soaking or kid-bathing – will affect the choice of shape and materials. Should you want a whirlpool system, you'll need a molded tub in a deck-mounted setting.

The shower may be sited with the tub or given its own stall, but in either case you can place the shower valve and head at the height you want. Shower systems are either exposed or concealed; both offer a wide range of options and numerous technical features, such as thermostatic mixers, pressure balance valves, hand showers, various showerheads, and body sprays.

Floor-mounted fittings, *opposite top left*, keep tub sides comfortable for bathers to lean against. **Tubs take varied forms**: *opposite far left,* a deep soaking tub with a generous deck for lounging; *opposite above left,* a reconditioned claw-foot tub with vintage appeal; and, *opposite below left,* the sculptural form of a vessel tub. **Three options for built-in shower amenities include**: *top right,* a shower and foot-soaking tub combination; *far right,* a corner shelf to hold bath necessities; and, *right,* a handheld shower and ledge seat, which facilitate grooming and shaving.

Sink and Toilet Basics

Sinks present a tremendous design opportunity, with a nearly infinite array of shapes, sizes, materials, and structures to choose from: old, new, or repurposed; porcelain, metal, glass, or stone. Any vessel that can be plumbed can function as a sink. Vanities have closed cabinet fronts. Pedestals, washstands, and consoles stand on legs, which keep a bathroom looking open, and wash tables pair a basin with a freestanding table. Today's toilet also comes in a wide variety of shapes and sizes. There are long-seat and short-seat versions. Tanks, bases, and bowls are available in a full range of profiles, with seats in such materials as sealed wood and, most commonly, molded plastic.

When choosing a sink, first consider the height(s) of those who will be using it. Vintage sinks standing 31 inches high may be too short for a tall person; standard porcelain models, at 33 to 36 inches, may be too tall for a small child. You can opt for wall-mounted sinks at any height, or combine a basin with a customized base. If you have space, mount the bowl on the countertop. For the cleanest edge, drop it in flush, or undermount it.

Always check to make sure both hands fit comfortably in the basin to keep splashing to a minimum. In a high-traffic bathroom, the bowl should be no less than 19 inches wide, 15 to 16 inches front to back, and 6 inches deep. In a powder room, the bowl may be narrower, but no shallower from front to back.

When selecting a toilet, choose a model that flushes powerfully and fills quietly. U.S. federal law now mandates the use of no more than 1.6 gallons of water for flushing, a reduction in water consumption that newer designs handle better than old.

Sinks come in varied forms, *opposite far left, top to bottom:* a self-rimming pedestal with a flank of deck space, a sculptural vessel-style sink set atop the counter, and an oblong metal basin, undermounted in a marble counter. **A diminutive wall-mounted corner sink**, *opposite left*, makes the most of a small space. Decorative moulding hides part of the plumbing. **Rounded corners and a backsplash**, *above left*, give a porcelain pedestal sink a generous feeling. **A rounded, wall-mounted tank toilet**, *far left*, with a central plunging flush has a classic shape. A sculptural form with a wide seat, *left*, is more modern.

Faucet and Fitting Basics

Design has its roots in culture. This is just as true of bath hardware as it is of living room furniture. The French, for example, were the first to merge hot and cold water taps into a single mixed channel (though many Europeans still favor the traditional division of hot and cold water). In the United States, tastes favor size over ornament, with styles that offer flexibility (such as handheld showers) and convenience (control at the touch of a finger). Choose fittings based on craftsmanship – standards to watch for include solid cast-brass bodies for weight, fine plated finishes with no visible seams, and sculptured forms that fit well in the hand – and your investment will last a lifetime.

"Fittings" is the technical term for all faucets, spouts, spigots, handles, tub fillers, and other hardware that move water to and away from a fixture. Start with the faucet for your sink – routines and needs here vary the most – then extend whatever design style you choose to the other fittings. Tall, arching profiles won't interfere with the basin if you're bathing a baby or washing hair. Lower spouts, whether straight or curved, offer an increased rush of water but less clearance, and so require deeper bowls. To avoid splashes, make sure the spout is long enough to overhang the rim of the basin and pour directly into the drain.

Select finish and silhouette to create consistency of style in your bathroom. Standard metal finishes include (from cool to warm) stainless steel, chrome, nickel, and pewter, in polished, brushed, or matte; brass, bronze, copper, and gold bring in warmer colors. Handles come in a variety of forms, including crossbar, tri-spoke, lever, toggle, and pull, and should match the scale, proportions, and style of the fixtures.

A toggle handle, *opposite far left*, has a smooth motion that yields a highly controllable blend of hot and cold water. **A cantilevered faucet with pedestal soap dish**, *opposite top*, saves space at a small wall-mounted sink. **An English classic**, *opposite center*, the nickel crossbar handle and teapot spout have a warm cast. **A high gooseneck faucet**, *opposite bottom*, with elaborate turned pull handles, clears the top of the sink and permits a shallow basin. **Articulated faucet sprays**, *right*, allow the user to aim the water jet precisely. A handheld shower makes it easier to rinse the tub, shower stall – and yourself.

color

Color is a science and an art. In simple terms, the science of color has to do with light while the art of color revolves around pigment. But the art of color also deals with chemistry – the chemistry of emotion. It's a pleasure to find the different combinations of hues that create a happy visual experience and express your own color point of view.

Putting together a color palette for the bath requires special thought, in part because there is so much color already. The tiles, fixtures, and fittings establish the foundation of your scheme.

Most bathrooms contain expanses of white in tiles, fixtures, and fabrics, as well as in accessories like robes and soaps. White can provide a base that feels pure and clean, and allows warm and cool tones to harmonize.

In general, neutral palettes are classic, rich, and warm, and naturally work with the room's abundance of white. Soft or deep color palettes can create a sense of intimacy. Monochromatic or nature-inspired schemes (hues of earth, plants, sea, and sky) evoke tranquility. Vibrant colors convey a sense of energy. Building a palette of

To choose colors for your bathroom, simply look at what you love and what you love to live with. Discover the art of color and discover yourself.

Every color has, in a sense, its own spectrum. Each comes in a myriad of values – the different tints and shades that tend toward warm (red, orange, and yellow) or cool (blue, indigo, and violet). Green falls in the middle, which is why it combines so well with yellow or blue.

Also, when using color, finishes make a difference; surface reflectivity (matte vs. gloss) greatly affects the perception of color. In the bath, high-gloss finishes on tile, porcelain, and metal fittings can make the space seem filled with light. Matte finishes and hewn textures, on the other hand, tend to absorb light, an effect that can make the room seem more saturated with color.

one color in hues that range from light to dark creates a rather sophisticated effect called ombré, which can be enormously pleasing to the eye.

It's probably best to limit the number of colors you're working with to no more than three, or to develop a palette from a specific inspiration – a favorite painting, a fabric pattern, or a scene from nature. Be sure to paint swatches on the wall to see how the room's changing light affects them over the course of a day. Another simple trick to help you choose: start with a quiet palette and introduce color through accessories. This makes it easy to test a color scheme, and lets you change your palette with mood or season.

Water Colors

When it comes right down to it, the bath is essentially a room devoted to water. What could be more tranquil than to immerse your bath in a water-inspired palette of blues and greens? Bright tints of turquoise are positively buoyant when paired with clean, calm white.

Reminiscent of sea and surf, blues are naturals for the bath. Choosing the right shade of blue for your particular space, however, can pose a challenge. Let the quality of your room's natural light be your guide. Consider the time of day when the room is most often used. Most blues, especially those with yellow tones that are enhanced by warm light, are a fine match for rooms with abundant morning light. Turquoise, with its strong yellow bias, is a natural choice for a light-flooded bath. Its hue stays lively even in brilliant sunlight, and serves as a vivid reminder of everything aqua, from sea glass to swimming pools.

Whether you choose intense turquoise or another equally saturated blue, try using it on the upper portion of the walls, and make sure there's plenty of white on paneling, mouldings, tiles, and windows to lighten up the space. White provides a clean slate for color, and permits warm and cool tones to coexist in harmony, so you can accent a blue bath with colors from either end of the spectrum. White also gives a clean edge to fields of rich color.

Glass fishing-net floats, *left*, in the colors of seawater, inspired this bath's refreshing palette. Next to the chalky patina of zinc pots, they look like bubbles. **Color theory favors turquoise**, *right*, paired with yellow-based hues, such as the chartreuse towels here. The armoire has a full-length mirror and lacquered brass baker's-handle drawer pulls; clear glass drawer fronts keep towels in view, and in reach, of the shower.

Strong blues provide a solid base for accents in contrasting colors. Turquoise, for example, is a good backdrop for the sharpness of yellow-based hues (yellow is the most reflective color). When choosing accents, keep in mind that we perceive colors differently depending on their context. A blue-green will appear more blue if it's next to true blue, more green next to green or yellow. Colors also read differently under different lighting. Incandescent light tends to be warm gold or pink; fluorescent light is more blue, and halogen is the most balanced of all.

A zinc tray, worn wood bench, and marble sink, *left,* make texture as central as color in this bath. Semigloss paint, used on the woodwork, reflects light, and is well suited to high-moisture areas because it's easy to clean. **Soaps and lotion bottles**, *above,* add color and texture.

The glass shower door and the glazed tiles in the enclosure provide a sheen and reflectivity that enhance the crisp palette. The geometric border of matte aqua tiles high on the wall and tiles on the floor help to articulate the white space.

Handthrown tiles with a glossy surface and a liquid, sparkling quality add to the play of light. Highly reflective surfaces, however, also can create glare, so proper lighting and breaks in the color are needed to help counteract this effect.

Double showerheads, *left*, with separate temperature controls make showering together an everyday luxury in this built-for-two alcove. **Varied shades of green**, *above*, in accents from the horsetail grass to the glass spheres, serve as transitional hues between the bright turquoise and the chartreuse towels.

Color Palette

White, blue, and green is a classic trio, a comfortable combination of colors often used in the decorative arts. Turquoise, however, is outside the range of commonly used blues: saturated, intense, and happy, it's the color of swimming pools, semi-precious stones, and sea glass. Warm blues with yellow tones (like turquoise) are complemented by greens with similar yellow hues, like the towels here in a brilliant chartreuse tint. White, of course, is the great equalizer.

Materials

Wainscoting While this term usually refers to wood panels or boards that cover the lower portion of a wall, it can also describe full-height wood paneling. Wainscoting with beaded and/or ribbed embellishment is called beadboard.

Tile The glazed surface of ceramic tiles, which are made of fired clay, makes them easy to clean and can add a glossy sheen to a bath. The sanded grout used to install tile adds traction to floors.

Glass Made of minerals called silicates, glass describes a type of material with a liquidlike molecular structure that, when melted and cooled, becomes rigid without crystallizing. Clear or colored, glass allows light to shine through.

Refreshing with Color

If you love color but don't want a long-term commitment to a single hue on the walls, think like a painter. This room shows how a neutral backdrop in the bath creates a blank canvas on which you can splash color at will and make changes as the mood strikes you.

Suppose you admire brilliant surroundings, rooms infused with cerulean blue, fuchsia, or sunflower yellow. You may be equally drawn to subtle tones – taupes, grays, ecrus, and whites. Here's how you can have both. This bathroom has been decorated two ways, once in a palette of bright, hot colors, and then (on pages 78–79) in a modern, neutral palette. It's simple to design a color scheme for your bath that can accommodate a quick change, either seasonally or on a whim. The secret? Focus on accessories: soaps, towels, shower curtains, and even toothbrushes.

To begin, stick with whites, creams, or other neutrals for all the fixed components of the room. As the bathroom shown here demonstrates, this core palette will always be stylish and clean-looking no matter what you pair with it. Then, use color for those elements of the bath that are changeable. Whether you decide on a color scheme that emphasizes warm or cool, harmony or contrast, you can use accessories to vary the palette. Employ soft goods, displays, and personal articles just as you would use seat covers in the dining room or pillows in the living room.

White wainscoting, *left*, offers a clean canvas for bold strokes of pink and red. **A Victorian-era washstand**, *right*, plumbed for new fixtures, has an oak base and honed marble top that complements both brights and neutrals. Wooden bureaus also can be plumbed and fitted with undermount sinks.

A shower curtain is a significant element of bath decor simply because of its size. You can select a shower curtain for its color or for its texture, or both. You can use it to establish a textural theme or to contrast with or complement the room's existing textures. Here, the loose weave of the baskets and pile of the terry cloth also contribute to the textural palette.

Become a quick-change artist. Altering the mood of your bath is as simple as changing white towels to vivid pink or red.

Look at all areas of the space and balance your composition. Adopt the same process artists use when creating a painting: add and subtract color, experimenting with solid blocks until the balance feels right. Pay attention, too, to the way different materials affect color. Glass, plastic, and translucent, lightweight fabrics can produce a softer color effect or create a radiant glow because they allow light to pass through them.

A terry cloth slipcover on the seating cube adds a dash of color – one that's easy to change. Mount vases on the wall to bring in fresh color with flowers. This eye-catching approach frees up space on windowsills and counters.

Even subtle color choices can have great impact. A neutral background recedes and allows a rich, earthy palette – an antique vanity, woven baskets, sepia photos – to take center stage.

When accessorizing with color, you don't always have to go with bold splashes; soft neutrals offer plenty of variety to enrich the visual landscape. Here, the room has a completely different mood using quiet, tonal colors not far from the fixed palette. Wood finishes and natural materials complement this approach as well as they did the colorful scheme shown on the previous pages.

Enlivening this room's pale palette are calculated infusions of brown and loamy hues – sepia-tinted photographs, woven baskets piled high with towels and paper rolls, earth-toned soaps and accessories.

Here, a clear glass shower door replaces the colorful curtain. It provides a transparent layer that makes the bathroom seem more expansive and adds to the calm atmosphere of understated richness.

An old wooden bowl, *left*, once used for bread dough, now holds extra hand towels. **Natural materials**, *right*, contrast elegantly with the white environment of this bath. The baseboard and window frame are generously proportioned, which lends drama to the room.

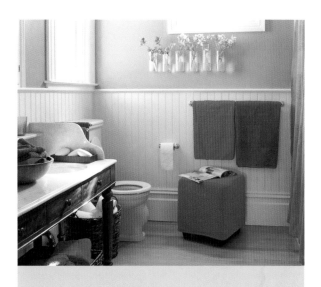

Color Palette

A sophisticated palette of taupes, whites, and browns for the bath's walls and fixed components provides a neutral backdrop against which the color of accessories can set the mood. The deep brown oak and white marble washstand, for instance, complements neutrals and brights. Here, tones similar to the fixed palette create a quiet mood. Chocolate brown baskets add texture and complement the rich honey color of the floors. Sepia photos add a lighter note.

Color Palette

Splashes of bright, hot colors against white wainscoting, taupe walls, and neutral fixtures animate this bath. Using a shocking pink shower curtain instead of a clear glass shower door transforms the room because its color field is so large. A hot-pink terry slipcover plus red and pink towels further enliven the mood. Even pink toothbrushes and water glasses pick up the color scheme. Limiting bright color to the accessories keeps it from overpowering the space.

Materials

Wood Using wood, which reacts to humidity and absorbs moisture, for bath floors can be tricky. Select a close-grained species like oak that's finished and sealed properly to prevent water damage.

Seagrass A fiber similar to straw that's derived from aquatic plants, seagrass can be woven into baskets and rugs. It has a smooth texture and resists stains.

Materials

Terry cloth This highly absorbent cotton fabric has uncut loops on both sides. One-sided terry cloth, or Turkish toweling, has the pile effect on only one side.

Marble Used for walls, furniture, and countertops, marble comes in a rich variety of colors. Polished marble has a glossy surface that reflects light. Marble should be sealed for use in the bath.

How to Bring Color to a Bathroom

While white always looks clean and fresh in the bath, there's much to be said for adding flourishes of color in vibrant strokes or subtle tints, in permanent installations or easily changed details. If you want color for the long term, think about the roles your room will play. In a bathroom where you apply makeup, green hues can give skin a pallid cast. You might avoid it around sinks and vanity mirrors, and use green instead in a shower stall. Use colors with percentages of peach or yellow to create luminosity throughout the room. Use complex colors – those produced from a mix of other hues – to create a softer effect than saturated primary colors.

A simple change of hue, *opposite bottom*, through the soft elements of the bath – towels, bath mats, shower curtains – easily introduces a fresh look. **Accessories found in nature**, *below and opposite top*, offer intriguing color palettes you can use as inspiration for selecting the perfect shades for your room. **Bath beads**, *left*, as well as salts, oils, and soaps can be colorful accents that are useful as well as pretty.

Containers and collections, *left*, can be used to introduce a new palette or elaborate on an existing one. Use multiple elements within a collection to explore the range of available tints and shades in one color family, or mix different colors within the group to create a zesty bouquet. **Tiles**, *right*, are a more permanent means of bringing color to the bath. Different styles, sizes, shapes, and materials create extraordinary options. Glass mosaic tiles, like those shown here, can add a liquid quality to walls and other bath surfaces.

How to Choose Color

Color affects mood and the perception of space. Light colors, pastels, and neutrals tend to make spaces feel more expansive. Dark colors, on the other hand, tend to make spaces feel smaller, and while they can be very dramatic, they're not for everyone. Shiny surfaces make color appear lighter than matte surfaces. Because there are so many variables, it's best to experiment with a few shades before choosing a room color. Select hues that make you look and feel wonderful. Then, view test swatches under various types of illumination over the course of a day to see which ones work in your room.

Reflective colors, *opposite*, like the light yellow on the walls, make a room glow. **Warm colors**, *right*, such as deep yellow and amber, make a space feel embracing. **Cool colors**, *below*, on the other hand, tend to be more crisp. Lavenders and pale light blues are particularly serene. **Deep hues**, *below right*, instill a sense of drama and can give a bathroom an Old World character.

Find Your Style A select guide to choosing and using the best

Warm wall colors

We've selected this sampling of warm wall colors as ideal choices for a bath environment. In this room, the skin's appearance reflects surrounding colors, so warm tones, especially peaches and roses, are flattering. Warm colors include reds, oranges, yellows, and even some rosy violets. Some warm colors have blue undertones and seem cooler; others have yellow undertones and feel warmer. Note that the type and color of bathroom lighting can affect the perception of color.

Neutral wall colors

This small selection of neutral wall colors includes a range of whites, straws, and greys, plus natural shades of brown from sand to taupe. Although white is most common in the bath (and the easiest to coordinate with other hues) these neutral shades are also very accommodating to accent colors.

Cool wall colors

Our sampling of cool wall colors for the bath includes paler tones of greens and blues in their various shades, from celery to lemongrass, aqua to fog blue. As with warm colors, these cool hues have undertones that can make them appear warmer or cooler. Blue works well with other colors and is an especially good match with white; it's easy on the eyes, and in the bath it suggests water and sky. Cool wall colors can be very flattering, but they must be carefully selected to complement skin tones.

wall, furnishing, and accent colors for your bathroom

How to coordinate colors

We've created this guide to help you choose colors for furnishings and accessories. By using core or basic colors for foundation pieces and layering in coordinating accessories in basic or accent hues, you can easily create a sophisticated palette in your bathroom.

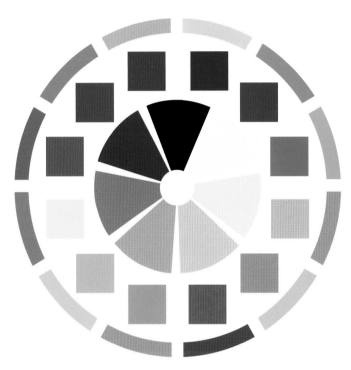

Core colors are the neutral shades shown in the middle of the ring that can provide a bathroom's color foundation. These tones are easy to work with; they can create a clean, crisp background, or function as a simple, quiet palette. Neutrals, especially white, are widely used for fixtures, ceilings, trim, and tiles.

Basic colors, shown in the second ring, are ideal for key pieces like furniture and built-ins, but work equally well as accent tones. To build a palette, choose a core color and then add a basic color from this ring (and accents from the next). Classic combinations include white and blue, taupe and red, beige and green.

Accent colors, shown in the outer ring, are ones you can use on small details to change the room's style with fashion and the season. Use accessories to bring in in these brighter hues. Make a warm palette pop with pink or orange. Add vibrant yellow to an amber color scheme, or bright lime to a green one.

texture

Texture comes from the Latin verb "to weave," which is exactly how texture works best in a room – woven through its design and surfaces. We think of texture in terms of surface quality: polished or hewn, smooth or rough, craggy or fine, tight or loose, soft or coarse. Texture also can be thought of in terms of depth, the ruggedness of its grain or the height of its pile, whether tufted or plush. All these types of surfaces, whether found in nature or in things made by man, contribute significantly to the overall design and feel of any room.

Along with the bedroom, the bathroom is the place in the house where we are on most intimate terms with the materials that surround us. Think about the way your body responds to various textures – the feel of surfaces underfoot, in the hand, against the back, or on the cheek.

Safety is an important consideration here. Some textures become slippery when wet, others don't. Especially when children share the bath, choose textures that create traction. For solid footing, pave floors with two- or three-inch square ceramic or unglazed tiles with plenty of grout.

In the bath, texture rules. In a room where you bare yourself, choose textures to soothe and pamper delicate skin; make surfaces inviting to the touch.

Light and color affect texture. Smooth and shiny surfaces reflect light; matte and rough surfaces absorb it. Reflective surfaces make colors appear lighter than the same hue on a matte or coarse-grained surface. Variegated color (or light and shadow) can create an illusion of texture, as can pattern. Use these attributes of texture to establish visual rhythm throughout your bathroom.

Think of texture as another palette that you can use in the space. Some of the same terms that describe color also apply to texture: subtle or bold, contrasting or complementary. Explore texture and highlight it to create a decorative, interesting, and sensual environment.

If you're not starting the room from scratch, much of your bath's primary palette of textures is probably already set, established through its fittings, fixtures, and surface materials on walls, floors, and counters. Tiles of all types supply texture, as do materials and finishes on bead-board and other paneling, porcelain, stone, and metal. To balance the bath's many hard surfaces, surround yourself with softer materials: chenille, terry cloth, velvet, and cotton. Since texture is relative, make smooth surfaces more inviting by contrasting them with rough ones. The bath is, after all, a room where we touch as well as look. Choose textures that beckon.

A Textured Bath

If you have a passion for texture, indulge it. Choreograph the decor of your bath by using a wealth of rich patterns and materials layered over different surfaces. A stimulating variety of textures in the bathroom wakes up and delights the body, the eye, and the mind.

One rule of thumb in design is that texture and color share an inverse relationship. The more color you use, the less texture is apparent; the less color dominates, the more texture draws your attention.

Exceptional stone or tile surfaces in a bathroom are a natural foundation for a decor that favors texture. Beginning with bold strokes on the room's broadest expanses – the floors and walls – you can style a space from the ground up to engage the sense of touch. Every surface in the bathroom offers an opportunity to be inventive.

The bath shown here employs elemental textures to conjure an exotic sense of history. Rammed-earth walls are designed to look centuries old. When paired with cast-earth floor tiles, they create a setting with a deliberate roughness and cool touch that suggest a blazing sun outside. Several layers of richly toned kilims soften the environment. The earthy, saturated colors of the rugs are in keeping with the natural palette of the room's walls and floor. Texture here is both visual, in the patterned geometry of the rugs, and tactile, in the raw materials of wool, iron, and earth.

Layered kilim rugs, *left*, establish a color and pattern palette. Their neat geometry complements the rough, irregular texture of rammed-earth walls. Rammed-earth construction is an ancient building technique used throughout the world. **A wrought-iron grate from Tunisia**, *right*, is repurposed as a storage system for hanging bath accoutrements.

Consider how texture changes in the wet-and-dry world of the bath. Look for textures that are appealing under both conditions. What welcomes the bare foot? What caresses the hand? Think through and touch every detail and accessory, from the mirrors on the wall to the towels near the tub. Visual texture is important, too, in all its idioms, whether variegated, solid, or patterned. Here, the solid block of color on the teal armoire is purposely worn, in contrast to the smooth aubergine finish of the cabinets.

A collection of shapely mirrors, *left*, hangs in a free-form composition on a span of wrought-iron grate. Repurposing lets you think differently about everyday objects and redefine their uses. **A spacious armoire**, *above*, is a common storage element in older European homes, like the French provincial farmhouses that inspired this residence. Its rich finish is made up of layers of undercoats and glaze, adding depth to its texture.

To heighten textural contrast, pair wood with glass, wool with stone, rusted iron with gleaming chrome.

Color Palette

The color palette in this bathroom is established from the floor up. The kilim rugs introduce a complex combination of teal, indigo, purple, red, sienna, and terra-cotta, which repeats through other elements of the room, most notably the armoire and cabinets. This palette could also have started from the walls in; the mottled ginger of the earth walls provides a wonderful background for strong colors and complex patterns.

Materials

Kilims Originally designed for sandy desert floors by nomadic peoples of countries such as Iran, Pakistan, and Turkey, kilim rugs have geometric patterns that represent different tribes. Traditionally flat-woven of pileless wool, kilims are rich and vibrant.

Wrought iron Wrought iron refers to metal that is hammered, twisted, and bent into shape to create decorative and architectural elements such as this curled grate. (These days, "wrought iron" is often made of steel.) Cast iron, like the core of some tubs, is molten iron that is poured into a mold.

Rammed earth A mixture of earth, water, and cement is poured into molds, and tamped down to create thick, highly compacted rammed-earth walls or floors. Ecologically sound, this strong building material is a wonderful insulator.

A classic means of emphasizing texture is to incorporate antiques and salvaged architectural elements into a finely finished space. Here, the surrounding environment combines the touch of the handmade with the finesse of the machined. Smooth elements are introduced in layers: polished stone on painted wood cabinets, chromed faucetry paired with hand-forged iron hardware. The vintage tub reveals a sleek white surface inside its lapis blue–painted exterior. Antique amber and tortoiseshell glass containers reiterate the colors found in the kilims.

Handwrought iron, *left*, forms a textural backdrop to the invitingly smooth interior of a cast-iron tub. The floor tiles are adobe-like cast earth, sealed for water protection. **Tortoiseshell glass**, *above*, takes on new character when placed on a rough-hewn wooden tray.

How to Layer Textures

In the bath, a textural palette designed to stimulate and soothe bare skin is most desirable. The trick is to bring the smooth surfaces and the silkiness of water into harmony with a range of other complementary or contrasting textures. Flooring might be sleek, with large pavers of stone, tile, or concrete against walls in high-gloss enamel. Other textures create counterbalance – smocked velvet, the fine grain of wood, unglazed terra-cotta, woven rugs and mats. Remember that every physical texture in the room also has a visual character, and every visual element should be inviting to touch. Always incorporate enough soft items to give the room tactile appeal.

Wood, porcelain, and metal, *above*, create the basis for a collage of textures. If wood is used, select species with tight grains and seal the surface to prevent water absorption (concrete and some varieties of stone also require sealing if used in the bath). Bath accoutrements like soaps add degrees of texture and visual pleasure. **An old wrought-iron grate**, *right*, sets up a pleasing contrast with the sink's smooth, gleaming fittings and the room's rammed-earth walls. Most of a bathroom's fixtures have polished surfaces, in part for ease of cleaning, in part for easy draining and quick drying. Matte finishes, especially on porcelain or enamel, can add another subtle texture, as can distressed paint, wood, or metal finishes.

Natural fiber fabrics, *left*, such as grass cloth, cotton, linen, and hemp, bring textural interest to any space, whether as pillows or on the large surfaces of walls and floors. Their subtle hues complement most color palettes, and enhance the visual interest of a room composed primarily of neutrals and tints of white. **Find beauty in the ordinary**, *below left*. Copper pipes and rough fittings can have an appealing patina and sense of history that is nicely counterposed by the soft texture of fluffy toweling. **Natural sea sponges, loofahs, and textural fibers,** *below center*, offer a range of surfaces to stimulate the body – and delight the eye. **A waffle-weave cotton shower curtain**, *below*, lends a textured element to the bath. Towels, bathrobes, and even slippers made of terry cloth or other fabrics add cushiness to the room's hard surfaces.

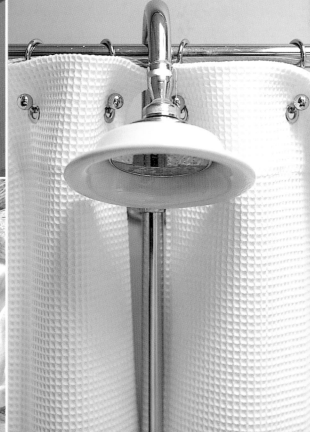

Find Your Style   A select guide to choosing and using the best

Soft flooring

Because of splashes, drips, and spray, every bath needs at least one absorbent mat or rug – preferably washable. If the sink, tub, and shower are far apart, consider using more than one bath mat or a large area rug. A mat is a safety feature, providing traction on a slippery-when-wet surface; it also prevents feet from touching cold tile.

Loop cotton Naturally absorbent cotton rugs come in a range of surface textures, including loop, cut-loop, and velvet. They may need a pad underneath for stability.

Polyester A sturdy synthetic fiber, polyester is often blended with wool or cotton to increase the durability of rugs. Polyester is water-resistant and washable.

Soft furnishings

Fabric always softens furniture, whether it's upholstery, a slipcover, or a cushion cover. Fabrics that are easy to wash and absorbent, such as terry and cotton, are useful in the wet space of a bath (water can stain some fabrics, such as silk). Choosing fabric for the bath is about touch and what feels good next to your skin.

Cotton twill A tight diagonal weave makes twill a hardwearing and easy-care option for the bath.

Terry cloth The classic bath textile, cotton terry has a soft and highly absorbent uncut looped weave.

Linen Woven from the fibers of the flax plant, linen is more absorbent and stronger than cotton. It has a pleasingly smooth touch.

Soft accessories

In the bath, softly textured accessories can soothe or invigorate the body. They run the gamut from terry towels and chenille robes to sisal rugs and loofah sponges. Natural materials – from silky, long-fiber cotton to textured seagrass and plant fibers – are especially well suited to the humid atmosphere of the bath.

Natural fibers Abaca, coir, cotton, hemp, jute, pandan, rush, seagrass, and sisal all come from plants whose fibers are woven into textiles.

Waffle-weave cotton Its textured, honeycomb weave makes this natural fabric highly absorbent.

Loofah A sponge consisting of the fibrous skeleton of the fruit of the loofah plant gently exfoliates skin.

soft and hard textures for your bath

Hard flooring

Hygiene is paramount in the bath, so hard flooring makes a natural fit because it stands up to the power of strong cleaning agents and can be wiped down easily. Look for nonporous materials such as glazed ceramic tile or tumbled stone, or use materials that can be waterproofed or sealed such as terra-cotta. Also take into account how slippery a material is when wet.

Ceramic tile Made of fired clay, ceramic tile comes in a range of shapes, colors, patterns, and sizes. Tile is installed with sanded grout, which also comes in various colors and increases traction.

Stone Alabaster, granite, marble, and slate are beautiful and traditional, but they can be slick. Tumbled, honed, and hewn finishes can help increase traction.

Hard furnishings

Because bath furnishings and fixtures must be impervious to water, they are made of hard materials, such as metal, porcelain, stone, wood, acrylic, and synthetic composites. While these surfaces are hard in the best sense of the word, they are finely finished to be pleasant to the touch because they come in contact with the body.

Wood Whether painted or natural, sealed wood is a durable option for bath cabinetry and furniture.

Porcelain The classic material for bathtubs, sinks, and toilets, nonporous ceramic adds sheen and is easy to clean.

Chrome A hard metallic element that takes a high polish, chrome plating is used to prevent corrosion.

Hard accessories

Accessories such as storage containers come in a wide range of shapes, sizes, and materials that are suitable for use in the bath. Everything from toothbrushes and toothbrush holders to soap dishes, towel bars, bath-salt containers, shampoo dispensers, fragrance bottles, and flower vases can add color and texture.

Glass Because you can see what's in them even when they're colored, glass vessels are useful organizers.

Ceramics Porcelain, stoneware, and earthenware containers provide opaque storage in a range of glazed and unfinished textures.

Wicker Made from flexible twigs or branches, wicker is popular for baskets and storage containers.

furnishings

Like any other area of the house, a bath welcomes fine furnishings. A furnished bathroom is a place where you can close the door on the world for a while and relax. Ideally, we'd all love to have a bathroom that has soft places to sit and lounge, to daydream, to sip a cup of tea. Even if you don't have that much space, you still need surfaces for setting drinks and books, and storing (and displaying) all of those beautiful and idiosyncratic accoutrements of the bath, the little items that are part of grooming and that satisfy the senses.

space and add character. Bring in the style of pieces you've used in other areas of the house, especially if you'd like views through doorways to reveal a consistency of spirit and decor.

Try arranging bath furniture to define zones: wet and dry, for example, or different areas for kids and parents. Begin, if possible, by separating the working parts of your bath (those areas where you probably want privacy, such as the toilet, the tub, and the shower) from the areas you plan to use as a spa or dressing room. Then, think in terms of style, comfort, and care.

Today's baths are retreats designed to refresh the body and relax the spirit. To make yours a blissful setting, begin with the luxury of furnishings.

It doesn't take much to make a bathroom special. Adding a few simple pieces can make it more comfortable. A vintage vanity stool reupholstered in terry cloth, a side table for books or topped with candles, lotions, and bath salts, even a spare dining chair piled high with towels can transform a space. If you can, incorporate a small cupboard or bureau for linens. Freestanding furniture offers amenities equal to built-ins, and it makes a space feel more sumptuous.

If you have the luxury of doing more, choose furniture that invites lounging. Sofas, comfortable chairs, and chaise longues are wonderful additions to a bathroom. They customize your

When choosing bath upholstery fabrics, look for materials that are absorbent, stain resistant, easy to maintain in humidity, and long-wearing. Chenille and terry cloth, for example, look stylish on seating and, just like your favorite bathrobe, they feel wonderfully luxurious against the skin.

A furnished bath offers escape and a break from the stresses that come with life's hectic pace. Furnishings can make a bathroom a peaceful retreat as well as an attractive bathing space. Opt for a grand spread if there's room – or a little flourish if there's not. Find ways to incorporate items, large or small, that appeal to your senses and provide comfort and personality.

Furnishing a Home Spa

What could be better than a rejuvenating soaking space that shares the best features of bath, lounge, and spa? Adding comfortable amenities to a bathroom brings elements of the spa experience home, and makes the bath a luxurious and inviting destination.

For domestic bliss, there's nothing quite like a bath fitted out as a spa. We tend to consider the bath – fully furnished or not – as a functional space, meant only for private use. Instead, try thinking of it as a room for living and relaxing, and possibly for sharing conversation with a family member or close friend. In Japan, the tradition of enjoying communal soaks in deep, steaming tubs has been practiced for centuries. Today, home baths are growing larger and more luxurious as more people strive to bring the delights of the spa experience into their daily lives.

Ideally, place a spa space in a separate room, away from areas where more privacy is preferred. Make your tub a focal point of the room – the area that people can use together or individually – and construct a spa environment around it. In this bath, a Japanese soaking tub becomes the central focus for a family who appreciates the sophisticated simplicity of Japanese design. If your space is more limited, a whirlpool, hot tub, or large-scale bathtub can serve as the centerpiece. The addition of seating – a built-in bench along the window, perhaps, or a chaise longue tucked in the corner – makes a bath a comfortable gathering place.

Bath teas and herbs, *left*, are essential home spa de-stressing ingredients. **A traditional soaking tub**, *right*, makes it possible to experience therapeutic bathing, which has been proven to reduce joint and muscle stress. This Japanese-style hardwood tub and deck surround are constructed of cedar.

A traditional Japanese soaking tub, or *ofuro,* is constructed with hardwoods like cedar using centuries-old joinery and woodworking techniques. If your bathroom is smaller than this one, look for modern tubs that fit one or two people, or even a double-ended soaking tub. If possible, include a generous deck surround (with a waterproof finish) in your plan, to let bathers lounge after a long soak, and to accommodate pillows and towels as well as bath infusions, incense, and other spa supplies.

Apothecary jars, *above*, are filled with aromatic herbs that purify, relax, and energize the body: orris root, lavender, rosebuds, and lemon verbena, plus bath tea bags, kept within reach for tossing into the tub. **Washable twill and terry slipcovers**, *right*, suit a spa environment. Posts made of Douglas fir frame the deep cedar tub, built with traditional Japanese woodworking techniques. A textured abaca rug on the cherry floor is a treat for tired feet.

Like any bathing space, spa baths depend on water-resistant materials. If you prefer the warm look of natural wood for furnishings or finishes, tight-grained hardwoods such as teak, cedar, mahogany, and redwood are sensible choices. If they are not in direct contact with water, properly sealed hardwoods like maple, cherry, and ash might serve equally well.

For sheer sensual gratification, a furnished bath offers numerous possibilities. For example, there's nothing quite like the unexpected pleasure of finding smooth wood and soft pillows in a room where chrome and cool tile are the norm. Imagine the luxury of a terry-upholstered chaise, inviting you to stretch out with a favorite book after bathing.

Take the opportunity to surround yourself with an array of textures. Accessorize with sponges, smooth stones, and tropical plants. Bring in a woven rug for stimulating texture under bare feet, or a polished wood table for a surface that's smooth to the touch. Revel in the pure harmony of natural materials and soothing water.

Kiri wood trays, *left*, are wall-mounted to display fresh leaves; a Portuguese ceramic vase holds chestnut seed cases. **A window seat lined with pillows**, *right*, of velvet, pandan grass, and cotton lays out a Japanese-inspired palette of calming neutrals. Extra storage for towels and supplies is hidden below the hinged bench seats.

Make your bath a haven. Wherever possible, splurge on soft textures, sumptuous furnishings, and the little details that make you feel relaxed.

Think of an especially memorable visit to a spa, or even a well-appointed hotel, and try to re-create the aspects of that environment that you found so relaxing. Bring in aromatherapy candles, piles of exceptionally fluffy towels, or a tubside tray to hold a cup of tea. The details that linger are most often simple and sublime.

Candles and incense sticks, *left*, resting in a sand-filled wood trough, conjure the serenity of a calming meditation space. Aromatic elements complement the tactile pleasures of the bath. Simple, spa-inspired touches, *above*, such as a bowl of cucumber water, enhance the sense of bathing as ritual and retreat.

Design Details

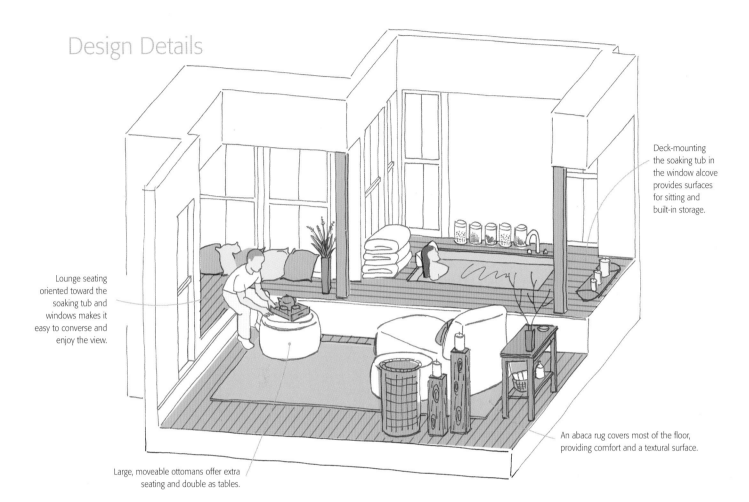

Deck-mounting the soaking tub in the window alcove provides surfaces for sitting and built-in storage.

Lounge seating oriented toward the soaking tub and windows makes it easy to converse and enjoy the view.

Large, moveable ottomans offer extra seating and double as tables.

An abaca rug covers most of the floor, providing comfort and a textural surface.

Color Palette

The Japanese aesthetic appreciates nature to the fullest. In a spa bath that's designed around an *ofuro* (a traditional Japanese soaking tub), it makes sense to select a palette taken directly from nature. The main colors in this bath come from wood finishes and natural fibers, offset by the white towels. In Japan, earthy, muted tones, in anything from decor to ceramics, are called *shibui*.

Room Plan

When a room has a natural focal point such as this soaking tub deck-mounted into a window alcove, it's only natural to construct the rest of the floor plan around it. This layout also makes the most of a beautiful view from the large windows. Spa baths require comfortable furniture, so splurge on upholstered or slipcovered pieces. Chaises are useful, as are oversized ottomans, whose plump, round forms can double as tables. Washable twill and terry cloth slipcovers suit a spa bath.

Materials

Douglas fir The very durable softwood used for this bath's upright posts is also used to make rail ties and trestles.

Abaca Also called Manila hemp, this strong fiber comes from the leafstalk of a banana plant native to the Philippines. Abaca rugs are comfortable and durable.

Terry cloth The classic toweling fabric, terry cloth has a looped surface, usually made of cotton, that is naturally absorbent.

How to Furnish a Bath

Select bathroom furniture with an eye toward improving function and comfort. Generally speaking, the needs of this space can be divided into two categories: storage and seating. Case pieces such as cabinets, armoires, and hampers are welcome whenever possible. Look for items with compact proportions to fit the smaller scale of most bathrooms (narrow curio cases and apothecary cabinets that are high instead of wide). Dressing tables or small writing desks can hold grooming supplies. Chairs and benches of all sorts fit in nearly any bathroom; add a small teak or other water-friendly stool to the shower to facilitate leg shaving, or a slipper chair at the vanity.

A tall, narrow dresser, *opposite top*, with stacked drawers is a perfect place for stowing bath supplies; furnishing a bathroom creates numerous opportunities for repurposing pieces originally designed for other uses. A built-in vanity, *opposite bottom*, was fashioned from two dressers, joined by a center tray, and topped with a cherry counter. Salvaged pieces, from old houses or even old hotels, are other creative choices for bath furnishings. A stack of towels, *left*, and beach sandals for visiting guests are left out atop a hamper. Fresh flowers add a welcoming touch. An upholstered cube, *below left*, provides comfortable seating at the vanity; its seat lifts up to reveal stored towels or supplies. A dark wood side table, *below center*, also offers interior storage as well as a display surface for a vase of calla lilies. A rocking chair in the bathroom, *below*, is a fine place from which to survey the outdoors. If you don't have the space, try a small upholstered or café chair.

lighting

Planning lighting for a bathroom requires careful attention. A bath needs plenty of ambient or general illumination as well as task lights dedicated to each station of the space. The room's lighting must be subtle and stirring, functional and atmospheric. It must be adjustable to meet the different demands of day and night or to vary the mood of the space. Well-planned lighting can meet all these needs.

Before you develop a lighting plan for your bath, study its terrain. This is one space where you don't want to rely primarily on available

Seek fixtures with translucent glass shades, because they reduce glare significantly and can help create a diffused glow. Pay attention to the direction that your fixtures aim their light: sconces can cast light in different directions, including up, down, and sideways. For a nice, ambient radiance, think about indirect lighting, which usually recesses the light source in an overhead cove (hence the term "cove lighting").

It's important to understand what qualities of light will work best, both with your skin tone and the materials in the bath. The goal is to provide

Well-planned bathroom lighting puts illumination where you need it. It also establishes mood, giving the space a sense of energy or serenity.

natural light; it's the rare bathroom that has sufficient windows to provide enough illumination for the many activities that take place here.

A good lighting plan begins at the vanity, and proceeds from there. The best approach at the vanity is to use both side and top lighting. Surround the mirror with clear, soft light to avoid shadows and glare on your face. Sconces and strip lights are suitable choices. In the shower, where space is often enclosed, lighting should be bright enough to shave by, day or night. Tubs also need adequate light; try a recessed fixture or a can light, and direct the beam outside the tub to prevent bounce-back off the water.

the room with a background of flattering, even light. If your bath has lots of high-gloss surfaces, use low-wattage lighting on the walls and ceiling to help avoid glare and to create a soft glow.

To change the mood of installed lighting in the bath or to add a decorative flourish, use accent lighting. Floor lamps, table lamps, or chandeliers can all function as accent lights. For further flexibility in changing the mood of any bathroom lighting, install dimmer switches. Nightlights can provide a beacon in a dark house or illumination for a midnight soak. And don't forget candles. Bring in pillars, votives, and scented candles to create a true sense of private refuge.

Room for Reflection

Light is both a wave and a particle. Take inspiration from this wondrous fact of physics to design a lighting plan for your bath. Wash the room with waves of natural light by day; make it a romantic retreat at nightfall with spots and sparkles of candlelight and crystal.

Be bold. Be flexible. The more types of lighting you use in the bath, and the wider the variety of fixtures, the greater your ability to adapt the ambience to suit your mood. Dress up the room for evening with chandeliers, candles, and accessories that sparkle and shine. Dress it down for daytime with casual drapes that let in lots of natural light. Add reflective accents so that light dances from surface to surface. This bath incorporates suspended fixtures hung with beads and crystals, and uses silver accessories to establish a mood more alluring than the business-as-usual appearance of a traditional bathroom.

Light and color are tools that help you shape your space. Different intensities and wide or narrow light beams can highlight distinct areas within a larger environment; different wall colors can make the light in a space seem brighter. A lush jewel tone on the wall, like matte sapphire blue or cobalt blue, absorbs light and remains a vivid backdrop, even in full sun. At night, candles and chandeliers describe their own magical circles, creating pools of light around the room.

Small, crystal-tiered pendant lamps, *left and right*, modeled after 1930s hotel fixtures, serve the same purpose as wall sconces, and cast their light much more romantically. They frame an ornate Venetian glass mirror above the vanity. The lights in this bath have dimmer switches, so the brightness of each part of the room can be adjusted as needed. **A votive chandelier**, *right*, is hung over the tub on a pulley, allowing it to be raised or lowered.

Some baths are equipped with large or numerous windows that flood their interiors with lots of daylight. If your bathroom isn't quite so generous, try adding dramatic, romantic lighting. Intriguing light fixtures draw attention and create luminous points of interest. They also give a space more presence.

Light is a natural luxury; good design helps make the most of it. Capture its flickering radiance with mirrors, glass, and other silvery surfaces.

Find bulbs that approximate the intensity and color of the light at your favorite time of day, and then use them with dimmers so that you can increase or decrease the level of light. Experiment by using bulbs of different wattages to create lighting contrast. Lower-watt bulbs produce a softer cast of light than brighter, high-wattage bulbs.

A large room dedicated to bathing wasn't always surprising. In some Victorian buildings, bathrooms were grand spaces used just for bathing, separated from the water closet. Here, even displays are dressed in keeping with the decor. Cake stands with glass cloches hold scents and soaps. The glass covers preserve the potency of scent in the bath's humid atmosphere.

Color Palette

Certain colors and color combinations are especially pleasing to the eye. Blue, for example, is a perennial favorite in the home. With silver as a companion and white as a contrast, blue acquires an almost magical appearance. An extraordinarily stable, pure blue pigment discovered by Thénard in 1802, cobalt gets its name from the old German word *kobolt,* meaning an underground goblin (cobalt was thought to be detrimental to silver ores). A blue and silver scheme is also a natural extension of the bath's metal fittings and the colors of water.

Materials

Crystal A word first used in ancient Greek to connote clear things like rock crystal or ice, crystal now refers to colorless leaded glass. Lead softens the glass and makes it easier to cut. Crystal-tiered lamps cast a romantic glow.

Venetian mirrors With hand-beveled edges and delicate floral etching, this distinctive style of ornate, handcrafted mirror is a specialty of Venice that dates back to the Renaissance. Today, Venice is still known as a center for glassmaking arts.

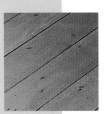

Pine This wood from coniferous trees (which produce cones) tends to be softer than wood from deciduous trees (which shed leaves). For pine flooring, choose old pine, or use a harder species such as white pine, a straight-grained wood with little resin, often used for interior trim.

Be creative with light fixtures. Just by changing the number of watts, the color, or the wash of light in a bathroom, you can create a variety of moods. Try different lamp shades for different qualities of light: colored silk softens and tints light; paper and linen provide a gentle, milky glow. Create a radiant atmosphere around the bath with candlelight hung low overhead and mixed with fairy lights at one side. Candelabra on the floor, below the level of the face, cast light upward for a glamorous effect.

Twinkling fairy lights, *left,* dangle from branches next to the bathtub, adding sparks of accent lighting. A votive chandelier is wrapped with crystals and beads salvaged from other light fixtures. **Faceted glass votive holders,** *above,* add sparkle to the room's warm glow.

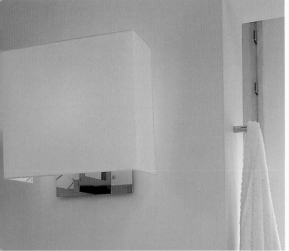

Ambient lighting

Besides providing overall lighting for the bath, ambient lighting can be used to control contrast, cut glare, and smooth out shadows. Ceiling fixtures, including suspended uplights, or wall sconces of all kinds are the main fixtures of choice, plus a portable light or two if your bath is large enough. Indirect fluorescent lights are useful, particularly for recessed lighting that reflects light off the ceiling (often referred to as "cove" lighting). Dimmers are essential for controlling the level of light according to activity – bright light for grooming, low light for relaxing at day's end.

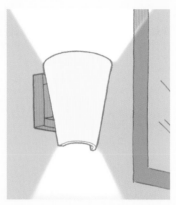

Uplight sconce, open top and bottom

Task lighting

Every bathroom has basic task areas to light – the vanity, the mirrors, the tub, and the shower interior. The amount of light you need for each task may vary, so try to match the light source (whether it's a sconce above a mirror, a makeup mirror light, or a wall-mounted fixture) to the activity. You can use vertical lights beside the mirror as task lights for grooming, or you can project a beam of light from a recessed fixture. If you do this, position the fixture to reduce shadows and glare. Make sure any light sources in wet spaces are UL-listed for safe use near water.

Downlight sconce, beside mirror

Accent lighting

Use accent lighting to draw attention to display areas, architectural details, or artwork. These elements are often placed along the room's perimeter. Try using decorative candle sconces or beaded-shade lights to provide a relaxing evening atmosphere for soaking in the tub. An under-cabinet accent light can illuminate a display or serve as a nightlight. For drama, use spotlights (low-voltage halogen is an energy-efficient choice) or wall washers (recessed can lights and track lights are two options) to emphasize artwork or points of interest.

Decorative candle sconce

ambient, task, and accent lighting for your bath

Uplight sconce

Ceiling fixture

Suspended uplight

Uplight sconces attach to the wall. Sconce diffusers, which come in different shapes and sizes, can be open at the bottom, at the top, or both.

Ceiling fixtures are a simple, practical general lighting option. Pendant styles should be at least 80 inches from the floor.

Suspended uplights tend to reduce glare and provide a welcome glow in a bath.

Downlight sconces, above mirror

Makeup mirror light

Vertical lights

Downlight sconces attached to a wall beside or above a mirror provide an essential layer of task lighting for grooming.

Makeup mirrors often have their own built-in light source that can be switched on for shaving or applying makeup.

Vertical lights are warm, fluorescent vertical light bars that can serve the same purpose as sconces beside the mirror.

Small table lamp

Under-cabinet light

Nightlight

Decorative candle sconces often have glass votive shades to protect the wall from flames.

Small table lamps with beaded shades change the quality of light by tinting it with jewel tones.

Under-cabinet lights can be installed at the bottom of vanities or cabinets.

Nightlights provide low light for relaxing in a bath or navigating a darkened room or hallway.

windows

There are many different ways to dress windows in the bath. Choices include draperies, shutters, blinds, or shades, all of which modulate light in different ways. Windows are one of the best places to express your style or to effect a quick transformation.

Dressing a bathroom window requires a few special considerations. There may be just one window in the bathroom, shaped or operated differently than others in the house, and you may need to open it frequently for ventilation. Treatments on windows in the bath may be

look, variations on blinds, shutters, or metal screening panels keep things simple. Shades are highly versatile and easy to manipulate, especially ones that pull from the bottom up. Shades come in a number of styles, including pleated Roman, insulating cellular (honeycomb), and the familiar roll-up in vinyl or fabric. For less body and more romance, consider using sheer panels.

If your window is outside the tub or shower, you may choose to work with drapery, which can bring elements of texture, pattern, and color to the room. The shimmer of silky organza adds

Whether you want a generous flow of daylight or treatments that offer style and privacy, drape yourself in the pleasurable details of window dressing.

exposed to the elements from both sides when the window is open. Material choices matter here. If you prefer draperies or curtains, you'll want to consider styles that remove easily for cleaning and fabrics that won't stain easily, fade, or bleed color, and that hold up well to humidity.

Put function first: decide how you'd prefer to adjust the amount of daylight you receive (and how much privacy you need). An abundance of natural light is a luxury, but bare windows aren't practical unless you have a space with sheltered views. If you want the same amount of light and privacy at all times, consider installing panes of translucent glass in the window. For a neat, clean

mystery, while durable cotton twill suits a family bathroom. A small window might allow you to use a vintage fabric or special textile panel.

Hardware and accessories can accentuate your fabric selection and provide a finishing touch for window treatments. You can match the hardware material with the rest of the fittings in the bath. Bring new style to your windows with all manner of curtain rods, decorative finials, and holdbacks.

Once you've settled on a style, the basic rules apply as much to window treatments as they do to other aspects of the bath: don't shy away from color; if you do, stick with neutrals and bring in texture; and always, always, always measure.

A Seaside View

When it comes to screening small windows in
the bath, experiment with objects from nature.
The sea yields endless treasures for decoration,
even unexpected window shades.

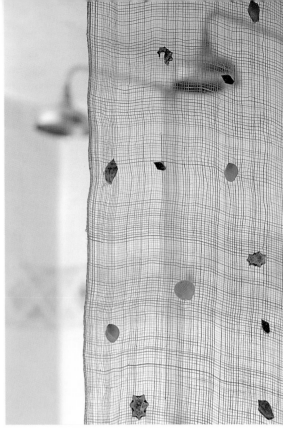

Beachcombing finds can be inspired
choices for the bath since they create
an instant association with sea and surf.
The sea harbors much that's beautiful
for use in the bath. A handful of sea
glass, coral, or shells can be fashioned
into a mobile; larger seashells can
double as soap dishes or can ornament
a ledge with enticing shape. If you
should happen onto something as
delicately veined as this sea fan, you
might want to set it into a small bath
window and watch it filter the light.

Sea fans perched in a window, *left*, establish
a motif for this room's decor. Hemp fiber gauze,
above, decorated with shells, serves as an outer
shower curtain. A natural sea sponge, *right*,
becomes a soap dish. At the beach, take care
not to disturb shells with live creatures inside.

Louvered shutters, *right*, and **Venetian blinds**, *below*, are classic options for screening windows, and are available in wood and other materials. Both adjust easily, permitting full or partial coverage of windows. Changing the angle of the slats manages the flow and direction of daylight, and allows varying degrees of privacy and visibility.

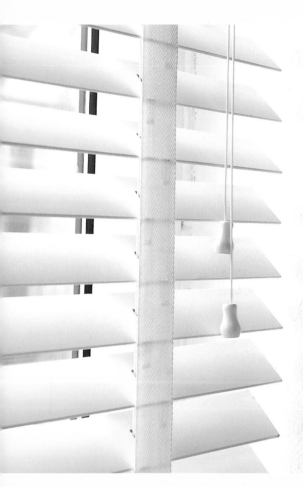

Panels of milky opalescent glass, *opposite top right,* or sandblasted textured glass are materials that permit light to enter while blocking visibility. **Striped café curtains**, *opposite*, cover only the bottoms of the windows; sunlight shines through on top. **Panels of treated acrylic**, *opposite right*, are easily bound together to create a screen that filters light, adds texture, and protects privacy.

How to Balance Privacy and Light

When you have windows in your bath, you're going to have to resolve the classic quandary of maintaining privacy while letting in daylight. Dressing your windows in fabric works well if you prefer to maintain a constant level of light and degree of privacy at all times. If, however, you want a system that you can adjust, take the architectural route with blinds, shutters, or tailored shades. These options offer possibilities for screening the bottom half of the window (shades and blinds that pull from the bottom up, or shutters partitioned in upper and lower halves) and leaving the top open to light, for the best of both worlds.

How to Dress a Bathroom Window

Drapery on the bathroom window can give you wonderful opportunities to incorporate more of the shapes, details, and accents that pull a room together. Choosing the right fabric depends on your own desire for privacy and need for light. Most sheer textiles filter light without blocking the view and look their best when hung in generous lengths. Other fabrics, such as linen or heavier cotton, screen more fully and can be draped and tied back to enhance their decorative effect. Window accessories, including rings, drapery rods, holdbacks, hooks, and tiebacks, add another layer of ornamentation to the space and another opportunity to reinforce the color palette.

A bar of soap, *opposite far left*, becomes an inspired curtain tieback when fitted with a length of cord. **A swing-away bar**, *opposite top*, mounted on the window frame, swings the fabric panel into the room, making it easy to control the room's changing light and allowing easy access for opening and closing the window. **This sheer voile panel**, *opposite center*, hangs from hooks set into the wall above the top of the window frame. The transparent fabric lets the woodwork show through, creating a kind of shadow box effect. **A fabric roller blind**, *opposite bottom*, shows off decorative window mouldings. **A round, mottled stone,** *left*, anchors a panel of sheer bleached linen. **Metallic gray sheers**, *below*, act as a fabric scrim, gently filtering light.

storage

There never seems to be enough storage to house the real necessities and little luxuries of the bathroom. But creative solutions abound. Start by asking yourself this: do you prefer a spare, open space, or a decorated one? This simple question nudges you toward the most basic decision when it comes to storage: built-ins or freestanding furniture. Built-ins, obviously, can do the really hard work of storage by effectively increasing usable space. You can have built-ins designed to occupy any area where conventional cabinetry and furniture won't fit.

survive the rigors of the bathroom environment. Many materials are suitable for bathroom storage finishes. Wood, metal, and wire need to be properly sealed, while hemp, reed, and rush function well in a wet environment. Laminates or composites offer great flexibility, and new technologies now make glass an option for bath vanities. Vintage pieces with weathered surfaces may not show wear as much as highly polished ones.

Never overlook hooks. Employing these very basic pieces of hardware can make the most of just a little wall space. Hooks are easy to install

Whether your bath is large or small, the truth about storage space is that there is no such thing as enough. Find simple, creative solutions that suit your style.

You can also specify fine, furniture-quality finishes or add decorative details to the cases and doors. Even simple shelving is easily customized and can make use of overhead space or transform corner space into working elements of the bath.

Armoires, historically, came first, at least for storage, and a trend toward freestanding furniture in the bath is once again gaining steam. If your taste dictates and your floor plan allows it, an armoire is a particularly elegant storage solution. Or, look for other, more unusual ways to accommodate your needs: a steamer trunk, a bombé chest, or a group of baskets or boxes. Whatever storage you choose needs to be able to

and are the best place (second only to towel bars) for towels and robes to dry out evenly after use. They come in many decorative styles.

It's your choice whether or not to put everything behind closed doors. Covered cabinets, drawers, and bins protect items from dampness and offer surfaces to display the things you'd really like to look at. On the other hand, keeping the basics of the bathroom out and within reach can contribute a visual palette all its own. Make a virtue of necessity and store toiletries and bath linens beautifully and in plain sight. With so many available options, you can find a storage system that meets your needs with style.

Storage on Display

Making storage fit is one thing. Making it beautiful is another.
The best bathroom storage ideas achieve both with the same containers.
Look for unexpected solutions that keep your necessities at hand
and add clever decorative elements all their own.

When it comes to storage, think from the inside out. There's something to be learned from old-fashioned candy stores and apothecaries. These were places where merchandise was always visible, accessible, and appealing to the eye. Keep this idea in mind when you choose a storage system for your bathroom.

First, take stock of your belongings, then seek out creative solutions that allow flexibility. Once you've surveyed the items you use (everything from bath towels and robes to tiny items like cotton swabs and cotton balls), and how often you use them, you can start looking for containers that meet your needs.

A pair of simple white bins makes an ingenious hamper solution for this tidy bathroom. Here the bath routine is itself improved by having one place for clean towels and one for used ones next to the tub. Storage is far more useful if it's near the fixture where it's needed. In this limited space, two small pieces provide more flexibility than one large one.

Plastic office file boxes, *left*, are assigned the new job of holding bath products atop tubside cubes. They're sufficiently opaque to play into the room's white palette but clear enough to let you find things easily. They're also unbreakable – a desirable feature in the bath. **Twin cubes with removable lids**, *right*, store fresh and used towels. When the lids are on, the cubes provide convenient flat surfaces for sitting and dressing, and places to set bath supplies or a cup of tea while bathing.

Organizing small, loose items into matching containers creates symmetry and instant order. Decanting liquid soaps, shampoos, and bubble bath into clear bottles or putting packaged items into clear containers (like the glass pantry jars shown here) results in a clean presentation, with the added benefit of banishing labels.

Be creative about storage. Stylish containers come in many shapes, sizes, colors, and materials.

One trick to unifying storage vessels with a bathroom's design scheme is to keep everything pale or white. White storage makes a space look neat and fresh, and integrates especially well if the mouldings and fixtures in the room are also white. If white isn't your style, polished metal containers (silver, nickel, and stainless steel are always elegant) reflect the palette of the room, while clear or translucent containers let the colors of the provisions inside shine through.

Towel rings, *left*, are mounted within bathers' reach. Sunny café-style curtains maintain privacy; the wood floor is stenciled in a harlequin pattern to mimic tile. **Pantry jars in a range of sizes and shapes**, *right*, like the classic pressed glass ones here, keep their contents well organized, easy to see, dry, and close at hand.

Some types of storage, like glass-fronted cabinets, occasional tables, and built-in shelves, can double as display. Clear panes of glass offer a convenient window to your belongings and a chance to create decorative still lifes. Combine large things with small, such as stacks of towels with a group of perfume bottles. You can also achieve a sense of transparency (without the constant need to keep the contents neat) by using translucent materials such as frosted glass, colored or frosted acrylic, or sheer fabric.

A vintage glass-front cabinet, *left and above*, reveals a well-planned organizational hierarchy of size and accessibility (big items on the bottom shelf, medium in the middle, and small on top). Space-saving sliding doors are especially welcome in smaller bathrooms.

Design Details

Color Palette

White, sage, and yellow make for a light and airy color palette. White enhances these soft colors, which come straight from the outdoors. It's a pleasure to see a vintage-style tub with a colored finish on its exterior and bright white porcelain or enamel inside. The yellow stripes of the curtains play off the white wainscoting. The floor's green and white diamond-pattern stenciling keeps the mood fresh. A subtle palette of paint finishes that range from gloss to satin further engages the eye.

Materials

Stenciling An age-old means of adding pattern to walls and floors by masking areas to create shapes with paint, stenciling was used frequently in early American houses. In the bath, make sure any painted wood surface is sealed well against moisture.

Wainscoting This term usually refers to wood panels covering the lower portion of an interior wall. Wainscoting with beaded and/or ribbed embellishments is called beadboard. In this room, the white-painted wainscoting and moulding provide a bright cream backdrop.

Ticking This durable fabric is made of linen or cotton, usually striped with bands of varying widths. It was originally used to cover mattresses for upholstery. Now the term describes a variety of striped fabrics such as the café-style curtains shown.

Storage for Two

A bathroom designed for a couple presents a unified front while providing each person with a space customized for individual use. Clever built-ins create continuity from one side of the space to the other, and keep a classically simple room free of clutter.

No two people envision the ideal bathroom in exactly the same way. When it comes to couples, a separate peace is often made with two distinct baths rather than one large one. Yet with the right demarcation of space, a his-and-hers bathroom can be a shared oasis. Opportunities for spending time together can coexist with having a place apart.

One way to make a divided space work is by creating visual unity. Each side then serves the needs of its user while staying within the style of the whole. Using a consistent palette of materials and finishes throughout helps to make the suite both attractive and visually coherent.

This his-and-hers bath has both communal and private areas that are defined by customized storage. Ample closed storage provides the foundation. A series of built-in pieces creates a neat setting where essentials are always within easy reach, yet hidden from view. Back-to-back sink vanities anchor each side to accommodate the grooming routines of each user, a necessary division in this shared space.

A cherry wood vanity, *left*, is built into her side of this his-and-hers bath. It features a moveable tray that conceals makeup storage; a slipcover on the chair adds an elegant note. The design of this bath incorporates two distinct areas, mirror images of each other, divided by a wall for privacy. A foyer at one end and a shower at the other connect the bath's two sides, allowing the couple to talk as they get ready. **Antique crystal and silver perfume bottles**, *right*, mix with contemporary containers and a silver vanity set.

Develop storage that suits you and leave surfaces clear for treasured objects. The design goal is visual solidarity, from fixtures and furnishings to mouldings and hardware.

Smart storage planning makes use of the spaces behind closed doors, with interiors customized for smaller provisions. The inset countertop of this vanity covers a shallow slide-out tray for makeup or jewelry. Drawers are subdivided and fabric-lined to protect beauty supplies. His side of the bathroom has a packing closet fitted with pull-out rods and space for suitcases. Each side has a window seat with adjacent recessed shelving to store towels near the shower while keeping them out of sight. Built-in cabinets above each dresser provide handy additional storage. The tall, shallow cabinets are painted the same color as the room, which seamlessly integrates the storage into the space.

Natural light is always a plus at a vanity. Although the configuration of dressers and cabinets delivers a wall of storage, the fine materials, craftsmanship, and scale give this built-in unit the look of freestanding furniture.

Even little spaces offer opportunities to build in details. Small conveniences and clever space-savers can have a big impact.

A side-by-side shower can provide a shared space in a divided bath. A common wet space can be open or closed, completely or partially tile-lined, and with or without tub. Here, using a double shower to bridge the gap between his space and hers creates a particularly elegant passage through the back of the suite.

Ideally a shared bath provides a mix of separation and togetherness. If you're working with a single room or a smaller space, use finishes, fixtures, countertops, and mirrors to define distinct zones for each user.

It's up to you how much visual symmetry you create between the two sides. Each person is bound to have different storage and display needs, though. If you want mirror images, you might build in a bureau on one side that corresponds to a built-in vanity on the other. For a sense of unity, use a shared motif in decor (like the shell collection here) to tie the two sides together.

Shallow glass shelves, *far left*, offer a small space for storage and display in the shower, as well as a shelf for soap and simple, refillable built-in dispensers for bath gel, shampoo, and conditioner. **Double shower heads**, *left*, make one stall twice as accommodating. **His side of the bathroom**, *right*, offers the same amenities as hers. Recessed shelving in the window alcove allows attractive storage of towels; a built-in bureau holds all manner of necessities.

An antique architectural drawing disguises the door of a recessed medicine cabinet on her side of the room. The gilt frames hide pressure-release latches.

Design Details

A double shower connects the two distinct sides of this his-and-hers bath.

Dual window seats create symmetry, and niches for storage underneath and on adjacent shelves.

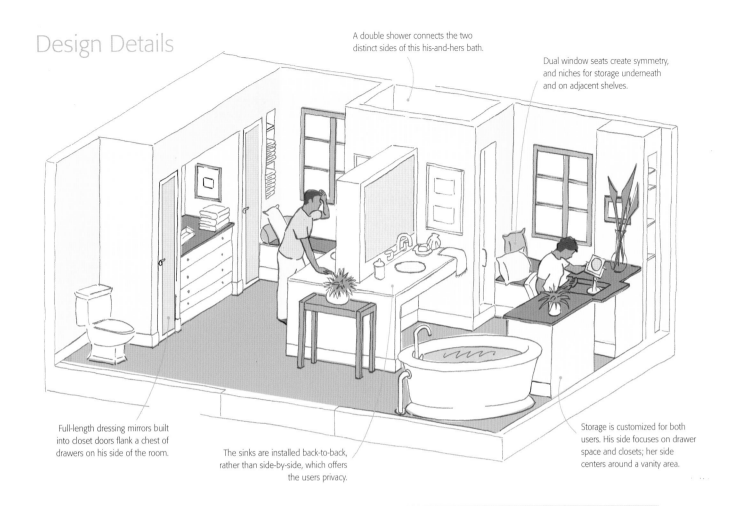

Full-length dressing mirrors built into closet doors flank a chest of drawers on his side of the room.

The sinks are installed back-to-back, rather than side-by-side, which offers the users privacy.

Storage is customized for both users. His side focuses on drawer space and closets; her side centers around a vanity area.

Color Palette

White and brown are the essence of this elegant bath's palette. Surface materials, like the cool white of the Carrara marble sink deck and the warm white of the oval tub, are interesting variations of white. Dark brown tones – in the knotty hickory floor, hickory-stained window trim, and cherry vanity tops – perfectly balance the lighter side of the palette. Gilt accents complete the color scheme.

Room Plan

In this his-and-hers bath, the room's two sides have the same layout and basic elements. Each space, however, addresses individual needs. Her side centers around a vanity with drawers for storing makeup and jewelry. His side has more closet and drawer space. Built-in storage helps define private areas; recessed shelving is adjacent to a window seat on each side. A foyer and double shower serve as places for interaction. This dual space is en suite with a master bedroom, walk-in closets, and dressing areas.

Materials

Knotty hickory The size and frequency of the knots in this hard wood influence how formal it looks. In this bath, the window trim's stain matches the hickory floor.

Carrara marble Polished crystallized limestone from this Italian city comes in many hues including blue, green, purple, and white.

Cherry The vanity tops are made from the dark, hard wood of cherry trees, which belong to the rose family.

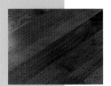

How to Make Storage Decorative

Storage and display can be two halves of one whole when it comes to bath design. Open- or glass-fronted furniture provides a union of the two. Rooms with open storage require organization, attention to detail, and maintenance to look their best. On open shelves, use baskets or other closed containers of various sizes to house smaller items. Multiples of the same container, or different containers in the same material, keep the arrangement looking orderly. The same is true for the contents themselves. From toilet paper to towels to books and magazines, you can celebrate everyday items by displaying them en masse.

An extra-long toilet paper holder, *opposite top left*, fashioned from a curtain rod, tackles the dual tasks of functional storage and creative display. **Wall-mounted open cubes**, *opposite far left*, adjoin a cube with a blackboard-covered door. **Glass-fronted cabinet drawers**, *opposite top*, display towels in crisp blocks of color and keep them within easy sight and reach. **Woven baskets**, *opposite bottom*, in varying shapes and sizes, offer visual texture and rhythm and give easy access to smaller items. **An ingenious open-backed armoire**, *left*, has a convenient pass-through to the laundry room and offers ample storage for clean towels and bath supplies. **Salvaged commercial bread-baking pans**, *above*, are just the right shape to store toilet paper, and offer a striking contrast of texture with both paper and porcelain.

accessories

Express yourself. That's the essential idea behind adding accessories to any room. In a bathroom, the choices are almost endless. Some of the so-called little things are actually crucial to the room's basic function. Others are there just for the fun of it. Of course you want to surround yourself with objects you love in this most private and personal room.

First, the essentials. Bath necessities can offer perfect opportunities for invention and creativity. Bathrooms require bottles for oils, shampoos, and lotions, and vessels for soaps, bath beads,

bold color or high contrast, or to layer neutral upon neutral and texture upon texture. As for the other small details – soaps or family photographs, bath beads or drifts of sea glass – delight in the fact that they offer the possibility of infinite change, and take advantage of it regularly.

Don't discount hardware from your list of necessity and invention – it adds sparkle to the bathroom. If you plan to stick with metal for towel and curtain hardware, door and drawer pulls, and shower fittings, you may want to match the materials, finishes, and ornamental

In decorating, as in life, it's the little things that matter. Remember this as you set out to accessorize the bath. For the biggest visual impact, think small.

and bath teas. You needn't stick to everyday solutions: serve your soap on the half shell (the one you collected during a beach vacation) or in the candy dish or little platter you found at a flea market. Use a bud vase, antique glass, or jelly jar to hold a colorful bouquet of toothbrushes.

Mirrors are a category unto themselves. In addition to size, shape, and number, consider frame style and material, including, of course, the mirror that's integral to the medicine chest.

Don't forget soft goods. Towels, robes, bathmats, shower curtains, window treatments, and upholstery fabrics all give you a chance to play with hue and pattern, to lift your spirits with

details to those of faucets and exposed plumbing. If matched sets aren't your style, you might mix it up for contrast: polished brass or chrome, paired with the more subtle effects of brushed metals or uncoated, oxidized-finish fixtures. Or add a few classic forms with decorative enameled finishes.

The options for cabinet hardware are almost limitless – glass, acrylic, metal, wood, of all shapes and in innumerable sizes. Use these ornamental details to add color and variety to the room. Or expand on motifs you have already established, such as shells, glass balls, or nautical ornaments. In this room of working details, even little things can play a role as simple, beautiful accessories.

A Botanical Bath

A bathroom is by nature a wet, humid space. Use the room's temperate atmosphere to create a glorious garden setting. Plants are the perfect natural accessory, and many thrive in this environment. If you've got a green thumb, the bath is a perfect place to put it to use.

Suppose you're a city dweller or you live in a space where a full-scale garden seems to be out of the question. Plants aren't much of an option except for a window box or a few seedlings on the sill. But if the desire to cultivate remains, it can provide inspiration for how to design and use your bath.

Be creative. You needn't look far for a chance to use your imagination, and to find ways around your garden limitations. No matter what size your bath is, you've got the conditions necessary to create an indoor tropical paradise. There's a daily shower, for instance. There are regular clouds of steamy heat and frequent occurrences of the dew point in a space that's humid by nature. There's high-intensity lighting, which you can calibrate to suit your horticultural needs. For all intents and purposes, you can essentially have a greenhouse in your home.

Accessorizing a garden bath provides interesting decorative challenges. What's suitable for use as a plant stand? Consider repurposing a wall shelf, like the mahogany wood one used on the floor in this room. Mahogany is a durable choice for bathroom furniture.

Moisture-loving plants, *left*, suited to the bath include citrus trees, such as lemon, lime, and orange, all of which have fragrant blossoms that release a delicious, tantalizing perfume. **Water hyacinth**, *right*, (in large glass vessels) and jatropha are other species that are well-suited to bath horticulture, as are many varieties of orchids and bromeliads.

Have fun with the materials you choose for your garden bath. Think about using earthier textures for your bath's surfaces, such as the Mexican terra-cotta paving tiles on the floor here (commonly called saltillo tile). This bathroom mixes and matches materials – integrally colored plaster walls, glass and stone containers – to create a sensually sophisticated and visually pleasing composition. The crisp white of toweling and fixtures serves to bring each hue and surface into focus.

The porcelain-smooth finishes, *left*, of the tub and sinks provide a visual and textural contrast with the plaster walls, tiled floors, and a hemp rug. **A moss "bath mat"**, *above*, is a witty accent. **The sink shapes**, *right*, were designed to suggest the whirls and spirals of flowing water.

Color Palette

Earthy colors like this room's sunny gold walls, terra-cotta floors, and green glass tiles are unusual for the bath, where palettes tend toward white, water colors, or the peaches and roses that reflect prettily on the skin. Strong colors can give a bath distinction. A garden palette suits a botanical bath, especially one graced by natural light. If you choose unconventional colors, keep it simple. Dark tones are good for the floor, while lighter and/or saturated hues work better for the walls.

Materials

Terra-cotta Meaning "baked earth," terra-cotta is used to make tiles that are usually hard-fired (whether glazed or not) for architectural uses like floors. Because terra-cotta is somewhat soft, tiles should be glazed after installation and periodically refinished.

Stucco Veneziano In Venice in the 1500s, builders added marble dust to lime plaster to create walls that looked like marble without its weight. What came to be known as Venetian plaster is applied in multiple thin coats. Today it is often acrylic based.

Glass mosaic tiles Available in a wide range of colors and degrees of transparency and opacity, glass mosaic tiles add a special, liquid quality to bathroom surfaces. Here, leafy-green square tiles line a shower enclosure, echoing the garden hues of the room's green plants.

How far should you go with the garden theme? The high ceiling in this bathroom accommodates small trees; in a smaller space, consider using herb topiaries. Keep the rest of the bath interior simple, to contrast with the lush greenery. Here, the toilet, tub, and sinks epitomize a contemporary, sculptural aesthetic. Plumbing is concealed, and over-the-sink cabinets are recessed into the wall so as not to interrupt the room's sleek surfaces.

Shutters over the bathtub, *left*, conceal a pass-through to the bedroom. The high-sided tub provides luxurious depth for soaking.
A modern, sculptural toilet, *above*, has the profile of a chair with an unusually tall tank that creates a backrest. The flush lever is made a shapely detail that complements the purity of the forms.

Designing a Guest Bath

In a guest bath, accessories are the essence of the art of hospitality.
Put out snowy linens. Provide each visitor with a robe. Cut fresh flowers
for a fragrant greeting. Use the little things to make your guests feel as
if they're not only welcome, but absolutely at home.

How do you outfit the perfect guest bath? There are
etiquette lists galore for hosts and hostesses, but you can
add lots of little luxuries without reading a word. It's easy
to make guests feel cared for: be generous, and be practical.
You needn't put in a spa. Just remember to follow the
golden rule and provide visitors with the same elements
you enjoy having in your own bath. Include large towels
and keep new toothbrushes and other provisions close at
hand so that they won't have to go looking for a thing.

The best situation for guests is an en suite arrangement,
like the one here. Even if a guest bath is down the hall,
however, you can still decorate with travelers in mind.
There's something especially friendly about a room that
mixes vintage elements with contemporary accessories, like
the demilune table and white cottage bench shown here.

Small gestures make a big difference. Put out fruit and
fresh flowers; both are classic signs of hospitality. Grooming
supplies, obviously, should be included: soaps, shampoos,
lotions and creams, thick towels, and a plush robe go a long
way toward making your guests feel cared for.

A stack of fresh towels, *left*, makes the simplest bathing space seem
elegant. For a guest bath, choose the most luxurious towels you can find.
Classic, hinged-top benches combine decor with storage, offering a place
to sit and to stow linens for laundering. **Travel maps and a basket of
sun hats**, *right*, are thoughtful amenities for summer guests.

Once you've provided the basics, think about what else your guests might like to have during their stay. If you're hosting during the summer, sunblock and flip-flops would be perfect. In cold seasons, have lip balm and moisturizers handy to soothe the effects of dry winter air. Local travel guides and maps are always welcome.

It's nice to be able to add some special little flourishes to a guest bath that go beyond the norm. Whatever amenities you include, think about decorative effect as well as function. Some people go for contrast; others like the serenity of monochrome materials. If you've got white spaces and want to add color and texture, bath beads and salts are a useful and attractive way of providing that note. They come in all sorts of containers, from colored bottles to attractive paper wrappers. Consider matching sets of refillable containers for wet and dry items. The stoppered jars in this bath look like nineteenth-century pharmacy glass containers, but they're clear plastic, and unbreakable.

Subway tile, *left*, is a classic choice for a shower surround, and adds texture and shine. The room's wood paneling also extends to the bathtub's deck, encasing its side. Hexagonal floor tiles feature gray grout for ease of maintenance. **An antique nickel-trimmed shelf**, *right*, offers convenient storage over the sink. Beaded detail on the mirror frame adds an elegant touch, as do the classic single-lever split faucets.

Be generous when stocking your guest bath. By providing thoughtful accessories you make your guests feel as comfortable in your home as they do in their own.

Design Details

Color Palette

You can add visual depth to a white bathroom by juxtaposing different shades, finishes, and shapes. Here, the white-painted mouldings have a gloss finish, while the walls' wainscoting is satin (or semigloss) finish. Offset by the vertical paneling, horizontal white subway tiles line the shower. The floor's white hexagonal tiles add more geometric interest. The creamy tan of the linen curtains and the plush terry cloth towels broadens the range of neutrals. Small accents of greenery in glass vases freshen the space.

Materials

Subway tiles These rectangular ceramic tiles, usually white, take their name from their resemblance to the tiles used on the walls of New York's subway stations. They're a classic choice for a shower surround, where they add a horizontal accent.

Wainscoting Originally installed to prevent damage to walls, wainscoting usually refers to wooden panels or boards that cover the lower portion of an interior wall. It also describes the wood facing of an interior wall (paneling). This bath's white-painted wainscoting adds subtle texture.

Nickel This malleable, corrosion-resistant, white-silver metal was the finish of choice for luxury bathrooms in the early twentieth century. Here, the matte finish of the nickel-trimmed shelf over the sink contrasts with the polished chrome faucets.

Along with the staples of a well-stocked guest bath, treat guests to aromatherapy delights such as candles, tub teas, and bath crystals. You might also scent the room with fresh flowers and herbs that promote well-being. Mint and citrus are said to be energizing, lavender has been used for centuries to relax the mind, rose is calming, and rosemary is uplifting.

An antique sink, *left*, replumbed for new faucets, wears a timeworn crackle of old glaze. Contemporary pedestal sinks can approximate the style of an antique while offering new options in color, size, and decorative detail. **A generous supply of bottled water**, *above,* is a thoughtful touch for overnight guests.

How to Add Defining Details

Accessories add the finishing touches that make your bath a pleasurable place to be. If space is at a premium, these elements must do more than just look good. Containers can house soap or cotton balls, potpourri or toothbrushes, flower arrangements or bath salts. Choose vessels of all sorts: the bath provides many opportunities for incorporating antiques and salvaged items. If you're looking for something different for your bath details, scour flea markets or even your own attic. Touches of humor, personality, and eccentricity frequently come in the form of things not originally designed for this space.

A vintage sponge holder, *top*, is jauntily angled into the tub so that it won't drip on the floor. **A wire bicycle basket**, *above*, serves well as a tub caddy for soaps and scrubs. Keep an eye out for salvaged goods that can lead a new life in the bath. **A shallow stone bowl**, *right*, holds a bar of soap encircled by stephanotis blossoms, forming an aromatic still life. Use flowers as accessories to bring fresh fragrance and vitality to your bathroom.

Lidded apothecary jars, *left*, offer elegant storage for bath soaps, cotton balls, even old photographs. Create an arrangement with several jars of the same size, or mix sizes and styles. **Wall-mounted glass vases**, *below*, bring a delicate floral accent to the room and a spray of color to the wall. The same vases could hold toothbrushes and toothpaste or other bath necessities. **An antique toilet paper holder**, *bottom*, advertising a bygone manufacturer, adds a touch of whimsy to the bathroom.

How to Put Accessories to Work

Accessories that are useful as well as beautiful help to organize the bathroom while adding a stylish finishing touch. Consider each of the room's basic zones (tub, shower, sink, toilet), and pick at least one accessory that will aid in the use of the fixture. Think of these items as if they were furnishings rather than just decorative objects or containers. An old-fashioned clothing rack can be used, for example, to hold more towels than standard towel bars and hooks. True luxury resides in the ease that comes from every part of the space meeting your needs.

Tub caddies, *opposite far left*, span the width of the tub and keep supplies at bathers' fingertips. The racks are often divided into compartments of various depths, designed to hold soaps, sponges, and even a book stand. **Sachets filled with fresh herbs**, *opposite top*, add fragrance to the tub and offer visual delight as well as aromatherapy benefits. **Low stools**, *opposite center*, are always handy in the bath, both as extra seating (even in the shower, if they're made of waterproof material) and as an occasional side table for putting objects within reach of the tub. **Small cubes mounted to the wall**, *opposite bottom*, create storage within, above, and below. **A scrolled bracket**, *left*, becomes an impromptu bookend, keeping reading material neatly organized. Salvaged architectural elements can provide decorative surprises. **A painted metal quilt rack**, *above*, is put to work as a freestanding towel bar.

Sailing ships, *right*, are a shared motif in this collage of paintings and prints. Walls are a seemingly obvious choice when it comes to carving out display space, but many people overlook their potential in bathrooms. Collections of photos or prints like this can give even a tiny bathroom presence. Here, the subject matter is kept all in the same family, so it unifies the differently matted and framed pieces. **A garden trellis**, *below*, commonly used for arranging trailing greens like ivy, makes a striking wall display and functions as a holder for rolled towels and reading material.

How to Put Accessories on Display

Accessories and personal touches can turn an unremarkable space into a distinguished one. Sometimes you need to be creative in finding space to display accessories, especially in the bath. Possibilities exist where you might not expect, so look closely at all available horizontal surfaces and wall areas. Don't hesitate to bring in elements commonly used in other areas of the house or garden. Where surface space is at an absolute minimum, work on the art of arrangement. Focus special attention on a few beautiful objects, and layer elements of different sizes and shapes. A little surprise is, after all, a wonderful thing.

This decorative glass jar, *left*, may have been designed to display candies in a shop, but it now holds a collection of personal mementos. Layer elements to create an appealing effect. With space at a premium, use all available surfaces for display, including radiator covers and the tops of toilet tanks. When displaying objects on top of a radiator, make sure they won't be damaged by heat. **A photo display atop a toilet**, *above*, shows off a collage of baby pictures in a variety of frame shapes, sizes, and styles.

How to Choose a Mirror for the Bath

A mirror is as essential to a functioning bathroom as a sink or toilet. Whether you use yours for daily grooming, as ornament, as the face of the medicine cabinet, or even as a window treatment, make sure you have a working mirror of adequate size for basic activities like shaving and applying makeup. The glass itself should be a clear, uncolored pane with seamless silvered backing. For skin care and other grooming routines, add a magnifying mirror; the best ones use optical glass at a 3x magnification, rather than standard mirror glass at greater enlargements.

A frameless mirror, *left*, has a clean profile that seems to float against the wall. Large mirrors can resolve problems of scale in a small bath, making the room appear more spacious and open. Allow sufficient clearance between mirror edges and fixtures for ease of maintenance. **A wood moulding–framed mirror**, *below left*, gives the effect of having another window in a small bathroom. **Mirror-edging**, *below*, frames a mirror with interesting reflections and extends the liquid quality of the surface. Glass and mirrors are natural complements to the watery atmosphere of the bathroom and help amplify light.

Mirrored panes in casement windows, *opposite far left*, seem to extend the room's boundaries while serving as a looking-glass at the sink. **Wall-mounted grooming mirrors**, *opposite top and center*, often come with extendable accordion or pivoting arms. Some feature a magnifying mirror; others are designed with lighting devices to clearly illuminate the face. **A tilt-mounted mirror**, *opposite bottom*, is adjustable and can be shifted to accommodate users of different heights.

Room Resources

At Pottery Barn, we believe that casual style is something you can weave through every space in your home, from front rooms to private havens. For this book, we scoured hundreds of locations to find perfect settings to create rooms just for you. We experimented with colors, furnishings, rugs, drapes, and accessories to find the best combinations for each space. The results? This collection of style ideas, which we hope will inspire and delight you.

Each location chosen for this book was unique and interesting. Here is a little bit more about the homes we visited, the style ideas we created in them, and the individual elements that make each of the designs tick.

A note about color: wherever possible in this list of resources, we've offered the actual paint manufacturer and paint color that was used in the room shown. We also list the closest Benjamin Moore paint color match (in parentheses) for each room. Because photography and color printing processes can dramatically change the way colors appear, it is very important to test swatches of any paint color you are considering in your own home where you can see how the light affects them at different times of the day.

A Simply Perfect Bathroom

This new suburban house is home to a bath with turn-of-the-century style. All of the bathroom fixtures are reproductions, except for the original claw-foot tub, which has been lovingly restored.

Space The white-painted lower walls are redwood tongue-and-groove wainscoting. A corridor, leading from the bathroom to the water closet, features his-and-hers closets. The floor is composed of small white hexagonal tiles. Double-hung windows by Pozzi. Architect: Billy Budd, Mill Valley, CA.

Color Walls (Benjamin Moore Whipple Blue HC-152 semigloss). Wainscoting (Benjamin Moore Winter Snow OC-63).

Furnishings Gallery entryway mirrors, weathered wood chest, and PB basic towels, all from Pottery Barn. Architectural salvage, 72" claw-foot tub. Signature series pedestal sinks by Kohler.

pages 14–19

A Family-Friendly Bath

The casual style of this bathroom matches its ranch location. The newly renovated, single-story house is a vacation retreat designed for a large, extended family who also likes to entertain guests.

Space The 23' x 23' square room opens onto a galley-shaped powder room containing six more sinks. Throughout the house, beams and ceiling supports are exposed. Designed to let children and adults wander in and out, a pair of French doors behind the platform-mounted tub also offers bathers countryside views.

Color Walls and ceilings (Benjamin Moore Whitewater Bay OC-70 flat). Focal wall (Benjamin Moore Tricycle Red 2002-20 flat).

Furnishings Manhattan leather armchair and ottoman, Charleston chair in twill, rattan baskets with liners, and abaca rug, all from Pottery Barn. Vintage wooden truck. Woven market totes with leather handles. Florist's orchid baskets.

pages 26–31

Zoning a Wet and Dry Room

Installed in a sunny, converted pool house, this guest bathroom is part of a small estate. The property, just a short walk from the Atlantic Ocean, features a guest house and formal gardens.

Space The 12' x 12' square bath has a 13' peaked ceiling, an exposed support structure, and a painted wood floor.

Color Walls and ceiling (Benjamin Moore Snow White OC-66 flat). Floor (Benjamin Moore Stormy Monday 2112-50 semigloss).

Furnishings Ariana chair in twill, jeweled organdy canopy, solid voile sheer drapes, frameless mirror, Essential towels and bath mat, quilt rack, PB Everyday towels, curtain rod bracket (for hanging shirts), rattan basket, conservatory lanterns (holding plants), and Henley rug, all from Pottery Barn. Painted wood table and child's dresser. Bronze-lacquered wood bowl. Ironstone tray. Crushed bamboo bath mat. Empire tub by Waterworks. Memoirs sink by Kohler. Reproduction Victorian tub fitting by Delta.

Display Paintings (near sink) by Mary Beth Thielhelm; paintings (near tub) by Shawn Dulaney. All courtesy of Sears-Peyton Gallery, New York, NY.

pages 32–39

Fitting Out a Wet Room

Sited to take advantage of vineyard views, this wet room is part of an informal, two-story villa. The hillside property has a gazebo, a guest house, and a walled courtyard with a pair of Italian antique doors.

Space The wet room is en suite with the master bedroom and opens onto a wraparound porch. The elevated tub platform is accessed by steps.

Color Walls (Benjamin Moore White Marigold 2149-60 semigloss). Floor and tub deck: green slate.

Furnishings PB Basic towels and Spa brushed stainless hooks, all from Pottery Barn. Painted wood steps from Pottery Barn Kids. Custom textured acrylic window shade. Bathtub, Berkeley System polished chrome tub filler, Chicago series cross-handle faucets, console lavatory, and custom lavatory fittings, all from The Sink Factory, Berkeley, CA.

Display Tumbled river rocks, abalone shells, and dried starfish.

pages 46–51

Creating an Outdoor Oasis

This mountainside vacation retreat has several guest cottages that are built on permanent tent platforms and two communal buildings. An open-air bath feels at home in this natural setting.

Space Located on a small porch next to the pool house, the bath overlooks a terraced vegetable garden on the slope below. A pergola covers the adjacent walkway, which leads to the pool.

Color Walkway and porch: paved in integral-color cement. Natural colors from surrounding flowers, including yellow "Autumn Sun" cutleaf coneflowers.

Furnishings Frameless mirror with hooks, Essentials towels, Marquesa tie-top organdy drapes, and camp lanterns, all from Pottery Barn. Feed-and-farm-supply galvanized metal tub and hinged-lid box. Chicago series lever faucets and fittings and Berkeley shower system with tub filler by The Sink Factory, Berkeley, CA. Sea sponge and bath accessories in a carpenter's caddy.

pages 52–57

Water Colors

This traditional shingle-style home overlooks ocean vistas from nearly every window. The upstairs master bath has an especially good view of the harbor, as does the en suite master bedroom.

Space Designed to feel roomy, the shared bath has a windowed alcove for the bathtub across from a wide double-shower. A storage closet and screened water closet flank the shower. The bath opens onto the master bedroom, which contains a breakfast nook.

Color Walls (Benjamin Moore Seaside Blue 2054-50). Wainscoting (Benjamin Moore White Heron OC-57).

Furnishings Vintage claw-foot tub with modern fittings. Marble-top sink console. Contemporary folding occasional table. Zinc tray and planters. Glass fisherman's buoys. Enamel frame mirror. Screw-top stool.

Lighting Overhead lighting, sconces, and decorative pendant.

pages 68–73

Refreshing with Color

The three-story Victorian townhouse, with a colorfully painted and gilded exterior, dedicates its top floor to the master bedroom and bath suite. The bedroom enjoys rooftop views; the bath is tucked away off a small landing.

Space This Victorian bath with a high ceiling was remodeled to make the most of the narrow space. Twin medicine cabinets are recessed in the wall over the sink; built-in storage at the entry is shallow and tall. Grand-scale mouldings emphasize the windows. Floors are narrow-board oak.

Color Walls (Benjamin Moore Shaker Beige HC-45 satin). Trim (Benjamin Moore Simply White OC-117 semigloss).

Furnishings PB Basic towels (white and custom-dyed), Sussex towel bar and paper holder, Maxime cube in terry slipcover, seagrass baskets, waffle-weave shower curtain (custom-dyed), and simple wall vases, all from Pottery Barn. Vintage wooden dough bowl. Antique marble-top washstand (plumbed with under-mount sinks).

Display Western series photographs, *Barn* and *Fence*, from Pottery Barn.

pages 74–81

A Textured Bath

This French-style farmhouse was constructed with rammed-earth walls and cast-earth floors, which give this bath a naturally textured background. The house sits amid groves of old trees and overlooks acres of vineyards.

Space Constructed using traditional European building techniques, the 18"-thick textured walls and deep-silled windows are typical of rammed-earth buildings. This floor is terra tile: 1½"-thick cast earth (smooth, molded earth) that has been sealed and waxed.

Color Natural ginger wall and floor color from rammed earth. Layers of paint on armoire: gold, teal, and aging glaze, sanded for a distressed look.

Furnishings Frameless oval mirrors, PB Basic towels, terry robe, and Marquesa tie-top organdy drapes, all from Pottery Barn. Geneva lavatory and tub fittings by Grohe. Vintage architectural salvage tub painted with metallic bronze. Wrought-iron window grate from Tunisia. Oaxaca pottery, Greek oil vessel, and turned wooden vessel. Amber and tortoise-glass accessories, and hand mirrors. Contemporary carved wood tray.

Display Blue acrylic on canvas by Anthony Albertus, San Francisco, CA.

pages 92–97

Furnishing a Home Spa

Designed by architect William Turnbull, Jr., this contemporary California house completed in 1999 has wonderful views – from the Oakville hills to the vineyards of the Napa Valley. This spa bath features a hardwood soaking tub.

Space The Japanese-style soaking tub (*ofuro*) was built using traditional techniques by Hiroshi Sakaguchi, Ki Arts, Sebastopol, CA (www.kiarts.com). The bathroom includes pocket doors with cutouts that resemble shoji screens. Architecture by Turnbull, Griffin & Haesloop. Interior design by Jonathan Straley, John Wheatman Design (altered for Pottery Barn photo shoot).

Color Wood tones: Port Orford cedar tub (wood from northwest Washington), cherry wood floor, and Douglas fir ceiling and column supports.

Furnishings Chaise with terry slipcover, tuffet bean bags, abaca rug, pandan and smocked-velvet pillows, PB Basic towels, rattan basket, and Metropolitan table, all from Pottery Barn. Portuguese ceramic vases. Antique wooden soap boxes. Indian springwood bowls. Aromatherapy candles in wooden trough. Tivoli radio.

Display Chestnut branches with seed cases.

pages 106–13

Room for Reflection

Steps from the street, this spacious Victorian townhouse has three stories and a hidden garden patio in the back. The house features ornate mouldings and 12' ceilings throughout, including in this jewel-toned bathroom.

Space Converted from a master bedroom, the bathroom is also used as a studio by a clothing and furnishings designer: the non-bath half of the room is a dedicated creative workspace, overflowing with dressmaker dummies and colorful fabrics. A separate powder room is next door.

Color Walls (Benjamin Moore Blue Lapis 2067-40).

Furnishings Mercer double-door cabinet, Traditional lever faucets, and Sussex towel bar, all from Pottery Barn. Vintage claw-foot tub. Venetian glass mirror. Antique blown-glass cloches and silver candy dish, pitcher, tray, and cake stand. Primitive painted wood bench. Cast-aluminum urn with dried lavender. Creamware footed bowl. Contemporary glass cake stand.

Lighting Crystal-tiered pendant lamps, votive chandelier, icicle lights, and taper, pillar, and votive candles, all from Pottery Barn.

pages 120–25

Storage on Display

With its rooftop decks, circular gravel drive, and expansive lawns, this house has a stately presence. More than fifteen rooms fit into its three stories. This bathroom uses transparent materials and the color white to unify its storage solutions.

Space The bath is 17' x 7' and connects to a narrow back stairway leading to guest bedrooms. The front wall features five windows and a nine-pane clerestory. Faux tiles that are 1' square each are painted on the floor.

Color Walls (Benjamin Moore Cloud Nine 2144-60 semigloss). Floor (Benjamin Moore Cloud Nine 2144-60 and Light Pistachio 2034-60).

Furnishings Nantucket cubes, Sussex towel rings, and PB Classic towels, all from Pottery Barn. Vintage claw-foot tub. Crackle-glaze wood-frame mirror. Vintage-style storage cabinet. French cotton café curtains. Acrylic index card boxes. Screw-top glass pantry jars.

Lighting Bronze stem pendant lights with translucent glass shades.

pages 142–47

Storage for Two

In a secluded community just out-side a city, this rambling house is styled after a rural French villa. On a slope overlooking a harbor, the house has a separate entertaining kitchen, a pool, and this elegant custom-designed his-and-hers bath.

Space The bathroom is divided into two 13' x 6' sides. Motion- and humidity-sensor lights and fans are installed in the water closet and shower. The shower is finished in 4" x 6" subway tile. The countertop is Carrara marble; the vanity tops are cherry wood. Floors are knotty hickory with window trim stained to match. Design by Elaine Hall Murray, CKD, Allied Member ASID (altered for Pottery Barn photo shoot).

Color Walls (Benjamin Moore China White, Interior Ready Mixed enamel).

Furnishings Megan chair in twill, PB Classic towels, and leather, smocked-velvet, and Mesa fringed everydaysuede™ pillows, all from Pottery Barn. Cherry-top custom cabinetry by Quality Custom Cabinetry of Pennsylvania. Whirlpool tub by Ultra. Bath fittings and shower dispensers by Franke.

Display Crystal perfume bottles, silver tray and vanity set, and shell collection.

Lighting Recessed MR16 halogen lights around perimeter of room.

pages 148–55

A Botanical Bath

This top-floor loft overlooks a pier and busy city harbor. The roof holds a garden patio and a small art studio. This greenhouse-like bath takes advantage of the room's natural humidity. Plants thrive and add natural texture to the space.

Space The bath has a door and pass-through window (above the tub) that open onto the master bedroom. A second doorway leads to a large walk-through closet at the center of the loft. Windows have bottom-mounted pull-up shades. The floors are unglazed terra-cotta paving tile (commonly called saltillo tile) from Ann Sacks. The shower tiles are Moroccan glass tiles.

Color Walls: integral color plaster.

Furnishings Modular shelving and PB Classic towels from Pottery Barn. Wall-mount sinks, Edition 2 vessel tub, and toilet by Philippe Starck.

Display Geometric collage by Cecil Touchon, courtesy of Sears-Peyton Gallery, New York, NY.

Lighting Light fixtures from Artimede.

pages 162–67

Designing a Guest Bath

Fields surround this two-story white clapboard farmhouse at the end of a hidden country road. Wildflowers dot its expansive lawn in the summer. This second-floor bath with vintage-style touches is en suite with a guest bedroom.

Space At the top of a narrow stairway, the bathroom has a quirky doorway and roofline. Instead of plaster, the ceilings are finished in narrow, painted wooden boards. Floors are original 2" hexagonal tile. The shower enclosure is subway tile. The tub deck's wainscoting echoes the wall paneling. The threshold is marble.

Color Walls and trim (Benjamin Moore Moonlight White 2143-60 satin).

Furnishings Cottage hamper stool, solid voile drapes, and PB Classic towels, all from Pottery Barn. Vintage nickel-framed mirror and nickel-plated towel bars and bath shelf. Period console sink with single-lever split faucets.

pages 168–73

Glossary

Abaca Also called Manila hemp, this exceptionally strong fiber comes from the leafstalk of a banana plant native to the Philippines, where it has been cultivated since the sixteenth century. Abaca is not related to true hemp, although both are used in the making of twine, rugs, and fabric. Abaca rugs are comfortable and durable.

Bamboo This hollow-stemmed woody grass is used in the manufacture of crushed bamboo rugs, matchstick blinds, furniture, and flooring. Bamboo is considered an environmentally responsible alternative to traditional hardwood.

Beadboard The most common type of wainscoting, beadboard gets its name from the regularly spaced bumps that are milled along the length of each piece. This form of wainscoting became widely available with the advent of industrial milling in the 1850s and was a popular feature of Victorian homes. It can be used on walls or as a colorfully painted headboard or bookcase detailing to add nostalgic charm to a bathroom.

Bombé Used to describe furniture, this term refers to having outward curving lines. In French, "bombé" means "bent."

Canvas This heavy-duty fabric is commonly used for manufacturing sporting goods, awnings, and outdoor furnishing. When used for drapes, slipcovers, or pillows, it brings a casual and relaxed feel to a room. Canvas can be made from linen, hemp, or cotton and is available bleached, unbleached, or in a variety of dyed hues.

Carrara marble This marble from the Italian city of Carrara comes in many hues including blue, green, purple, and white. Historically favored by Italian Renaissance sculptors, this luxurious stone is popular today for use in the home. Carrara marble surfaces can add classic beauty to a bathroom as floor tiles, vanity tops, or the walls of a shower stall and have the added benefit of being easy to clean.

Cast iron Sometimes confused with wrought iron, cast iron (like the core of some bathtubs) is made by pouring molten iron into a mold to create a decorative or practical shape.

Chenille Aptly named after the French word for caterpillar, chenille fabric weaves silk or cotton into tufted cords for greater depth and richness. This luxuriously nubby material is commonly used to make bathrobes. A soft chenille throw adds a cozy touch to a chaise longue, and chenille drapes give a bathroom a plush feeling of warmth.

Cherry A popular hardwood because of its warm reddish tones, this member of the rose family is used for fine furniture and cabinetry as well as flooring.

Chrome A hard metallic element that takes a high polish, chrome plating is used to prevent corrosion. Bathroom fittings are often plated in chrome.

Coir This natural fiber is derived from the husks of coconuts, grown in Sri Lanka and other tropical locations. Once removed from the husks, the fiber is spun and machine-woven into matting, and often backed with latex for increased durability. A popular floor covering, coir is tough, resilient, and more textural than other natural-fiber rugs. It is exceptionally durable, which makes it an excellent choice in high-traffic areas. The color of coir varies based on its harvest time.

Cotton twill Twill fabrics are characterized by a raised diagonal design and are noted for their firm, close weave. Denim is an example of cotton twill.

Crystal A word first used in ancient Greek to connote clear things like rock crystal or ice, "crystal" now refers to colorless leaded glass. Lead softens the glass and makes it easier to cut. Crystal-tiered lamps cast a romantic glow in the bath.

Denim Originally thought to be from France, this durable cotton fabric became popular in the U.S. during the California Gold Rush, in the form of work jeans. It is also a great washable slipcover option for casual bath furniture, especially in homes with kids and pets. Repeated washings soften it and fade its traditional indigo color, adding to its appeal.

Douglas fir A very durable softwood, lumber from this evergreen tree is commonly used in many aspects of residential and commercial construction. Interior applications include window frames, doors, paneling, ceilings, roller blinds, mouldings, trim, and furniture.

Empire style This neoclassical style of interior decoration (and fashion) was prevalent in France during the first part of the nineteenth century. Identified with Napoleon Bonaparte (1769–1821), Empire style drew inspiration from ancient Greece and Rome, as well as symbols such as the emperor's monogram, military trophies, and Egyptian motifs (after the conquest of Egypt). Other features include decorative painted faux finishes, wallpapers, plush wall-to-wall carpeting, festooned draperies, chandeliers, and damask upholstery.

Fittings This term refers to the hardware of the bathroom, used to control the flow of water to fixtures. Fittings include faucets, shower valves, and tub fillers.

Fixtures Bath fixtures are the built-in elements of the room such as sinks, tubs, showers, and toilets.

Flat weave Created on a loom, a flat-weave rug is smoothly finished with no knots or pile, like a tapestry. A wool flat-weave rug such as a kilim is often also reversible and makes a durable floor covering for high-traffic areas.

Galvanized metal Metal is galvanized by coating it with a thin layer of another metal (usually zinc) to create a protective finish. It is often used to make ductwork or items such as tubs or light fixtures intended for outdoor use. The distinctive mottled finish of galvanized metal can add a raw, industrial feel and texture to an indoor or outdoor bathtub.

Glass Generally made of minerals called silicates, "glass" describes a type of material with a liquid-like molecular structure that, when melted and cooled, becomes rigid without crystallizing. While clear and colored glass allow light to shine through, other effects are also possible. Sand-blasted glass has a cooler, frosted look while a semi-opaque glass diffuses light without fully blocking it.

Glass mosaic tiles Available in a wide range of colors and degrees of transparency and opacity, glass mosaic tiles add a special liquid quality to bathroom surfaces. They can be used to encase a shower stall or on floors and along walls to create a seamless field of color.

Hexagonal tile Multi-sided ceramic tiles, often white with black accents, were commonly used on bath floors around the turn of the twentieth century.

Kilims These reversible flat-weave wool rugs feature bold, intricate designs. Originally designed to be placed on sandy desert floors by nomadic peoples of countries such as Iran, Iraq, Pakistan, and Turkey, kilim rug patterns represent different tribes and regions. All are rich, vibrant, and geometric, and they complement contemporary interiors.

Kiri wood The kiri or paulownia tree is native to China and Japan. The wood has a fine grain and natural luster, and it is easily carved. Japanese craftspeople use it to make fine furniture, jewelry boxes, and a variety of household and ornamental items.

Knotty hickory Hickory wood with a large number of knots is commonly used to make bath and kitchen cabinetry. The size and frequency of its knots influence how formal it looks.

Lavatory Referring to a fixed bowl fitted with plumbing and designed for bathing and grooming, this is the design industry's term for "bathroom sink."

Linen Woven from the fibers of the flax plant, linen is possibly the first fabric produced by humans. It can be as fine and sheer as a handkerchief or as substantial as canvas. Lightweight linen curtains provide privacy while still allowing sunlight to shine through. Much stronger than cotton, linen softens with washing. Vintage pieces can contribute a sense of history to a bathroom's decor.

Loofah This type of sponge consists of the fibrous skeleton of the fruit of the loofah plant which can be used to exfoliate skin.

Loop cotton Naturally absorbent cotton rugs come in a range of surface textures, including loop. "Loop" refers to the pile of a tufted rug when the yarn is passed through the backing from back to front, then front to back, and the resulting loop is left intact. The loop also can be cut to create cut-loop cotton.

Louvered doors/screens This type of door or screen is fitted with moveable or fixed horizontal slats that admit light and allow for the free circulation of air.

Mahogany This valuable, close-grained hardwood varies in color from golden brown to deep red brown and is used for the manufacture of cabinetry, paneling, interior trim, doors, decorative borders, fine furniture, and even flooring. While many tropical woods are endangered, several suppliers are now managing mahogany forests in environmentally responsible ways.

Marble Used for home surfaces such as walls, furniture, and countertops, polished marble has a glossy surface that reflects light and emphasizes this beautiful stone material's color and markings. It should be sealed for use in the bath.

Matelassé This double-woven fabric, named for the French word for "quilted," has raised decorative patterns on its surface that mimic the look of a quilt. The effect is achieved through the process of weaving in an interlocking wadding weft (a filling thread or yarn), rather than through quilting. Matelassé will become softer with repeated washings and adds warm texture to a bathroom.

Mirrors The most common type of mirror is made of plate glass that has been coated on one side with metal or some other reflective surface. With their curved surfaces, convex and concave mirrors can add an element of fun or mystery. Mirrors can make a bathroom look bigger and can amplify its light. Unusual, antique, or wooden frames add style.

Natural fibers Rugs and pillow coverings made of natural fibers such as hemp, pandan grass, seagrass, jute, sisal, and coir add texture, warmth, and visual interest to a bathroom.

Nickel Malleable and corrosion-resistant, this silvery white metal was the finish of choice for luxury bathrooms at the turn of the twentieth century.

Pine This wood from evergreen coniferous trees (which produce cones) tends to be softer than wood from deciduous trees (which shed leaves). Still, it is a popular choice for furniture, flooring, and cabinetry because of its rustic quality. Old pine is best for floors. Another option is a harder species such as white pine, a straight-grained wood with little resin that is often used for interior trim as well.

Plaster A mixture of lime or gypsum, sand, and water, this durable, sound-absorbent, easy-to-clean wall material is suited to paint, wallpaper, or stenciling.

Polyester A sturdy synthetic fiber, polyester is often blended with wool or cotton to increase their durability. It is water-resistant and usually washable.

Rammed earth A mixture of earth, water, and cement is poured into molds and tamped down to create thick, highly compacted walls or floors. Termite- and fire-resistant, rammed-earth buildings are ecologically sound and suitable for all climates. Because they stay warm in the winter and cool in the summer (their thermal mass slows the transfer of heat or cold), they reduce dependence on non-renewable energy sources.

Redwood While any wood that produces a red dye is considered a redwood, the most famous are coast redwoods, which grow up to 360 feet in height. This durable hardwood is used in home interiors and exteriors, including the housing of spa tubs, decks, siding, paneling, and rustic furniture.

River rock Stones sanded smooth by a river's flow offer natural beauty in a range of colors and patterns.

Seagrass Comercially grown in China, seagrass produces a fiber that is similar to straw and smoother than coir, sisal, or jute. Its surface and subtle green tone add warmth and an outdoors appeal to the bathroom. The fiber's rugged durability makes rugs suitable for high-traffic areas.

Stenciling An age-old means of adding pattern to walls and floors by masking areas to create shapes with paint, stenciling was used frequently in early American houses. Make sure any painted wood surface is sealed against moisture.

Stucco Veneziano In Venice in the 1500s, builders added marble dust to lime plaster to create walls that looked like marble without duplicating its weight. What came to be known as Venetian plaster is applied in multiple thin coats. Today it is often acrylic based.

Subway tiles These rectangular ceramic tiles, usually white, take their name from their resemblance to the tiles used on the walls of New York City's subway stations. They're a classic choice for a shower surround, where they add a horizontal accent.

Sullivan, Louis Henry The American architect Louis Henry Sullivan (1856–1924) was an important influence in the evolution of modern American architecture. His belief that outward form should express the function within is neatly summed up in his well-known (but often abbreviated) dictum "Form ever follows function." Frank Lloyd Wright (1867–1959) was one of Sullivan's students.

Terra-cotta Meaning "baked earth," terra-cotta existed as early as 3000 B.C., when it was used to make pottery vases and statuettes. Its use as an architectural material dates back to ancient Greece, when terra-cotta roof tiles and decorative elements adorned temples and other structures. Today, tiles made of this natural material are a popular flooring option. Whether glazed, painted, or unglazed, they add warmth and rustic charm to their surroundings.

Terry cloth The classic toweling fabric, terry cloth has a looped surface, usually made of cotton, that is naturally absorbent. One-sided terry cloth, or Turkish toweling, has the pile effect on only one side.

Textured acrylic This synthetic textured material is lightweight and easy to wash. Window panels made of textured acrylic filter sunlight without blocking it out.

Ticking Originally used primarily to make mattress and pillow coverings, this strong, tightly woven cotton fabric features a characteristic pattern of simple stripes against a natural background. Today the term describes a variety of striped fabrics that have many uses in the home, such as for making curtains.

Tile The glazed surface of ceramic tiles, which are made of fired clay, makes them easy to clean and can add a glossy sheen to a bath. The sanded grout used to install tile adds traction to bath floors. Light-reflective white ceramic tiles have long been used for bathroom walls and floors. Inset bands of decorative, ornamented or colored tiles were popular in the early 1900s. For a time in the 1960s and 1970s, strong colors and textures replaced the clean white look. Recent trends favor a more rustic look with tiles that have a handmade appearance.

Twill This smooth, durable fabric is tightly woven, usually of cotton, and has a raised diagonal grain. Relatively flat, this versatile weave is a good choice for slipcovers or upholstery in both summer and winter seasons. Denim and gabardine are examples of twill weaves. Brushed twill is finished to emphasize the fabric's soft nap.

Venetian mirrors With hand-beveled edges and delicate floral etching, this distinctive style of ornate, handcrafted mirror is a specialty of Venice that dates back to the Renaissance. Venice is still known as a center for glassmaking arts.

Wainscoting Originally developed to prevent wall damage in heavy-traffic areas, "wainscoting" usually refers to wooden boards or panels that cover the lower portion of a wall. The term can also refer to full-height wall paneling. Beadboard, which has a regular raised pattern on the wood, is the most common type of wainscoting.

Wicker Created by weaving flexible branches or twigs from plants such as bamboo, cane, rattan, reed, or willow around a coarser frame, wicker is commonly used to make durable baskets and furniture. Wicker baskets and hampers offer attractive storage solutions in the bath. A durable material, wicker can stand up to a century of normal use.

Wrought iron Iron bar stock is forged or bent into shape to create decorative and architectural elements such as grates, headboards, wine racks, and balcony and stair railings. Decorative forms include Gothic tracery, plant forms, and classical motifs. Today, items called wrought iron are sometimes actually made of steel.

Index

Acknowledgments

Contributing Editor
Lisa Light

Project Editor
Laurie Wertz

Copy Editors
Kristine Carber
Elizabeth Dougherty
Lynn Messina

Designer
Jackie Mancuso

Illustrators
Robert Evans
Paul Jamtgaard
Nate Padavick

Indexer
Ken DellaPenta

Photography Assistants
Lajos Geenen
Christian Horan
Tyler Jacobsen
Anthony Lindsey
Matt Lovering
Rod McLean

Stylist Assistants
John Czepiel
Curtis Speer

Lead Merchandise Coordinator
Joshua Young

Merchandise Coordinators
Max Baloian
Matt Blankenzee
L. A. Daniels
Catherine Dill
C. J. Rosseler
Roger Smoothy
Joey Tosi

Weldon Owen thanks the photography and editorial teams for their creativity and stamina in producing this book and acknowledges the following people and organizations for their invaluable contribution in:

Allowing us to photograph their wonderful homes
Howard & Lori Backen, Karen Barbour & David Sheff, Ken & Shelley Bovero, Thornton Carlyle Bunch, Jr., & Marjorie Caldwell, Ken Burnet, Susan Burnet, & Gregory Nemrow at Gaige House Inn, Catherine Chermayeff, David Easton & Cynthia Wright, Robert & Kelli Glazier, Sam & Diana Hunt, Leslie Murdock, Elaine & Hall Murray, Timothy O'Brien, Jim & Joan Reiher, Rod Rougelot, Tom & Linda Scheibal, Jon Staub, Celia Tejada, and Stephen & Kelly Willrich

Supplying artwork
Anthony Albertus, Gaines Petyon, and Celia Tejada. Courtesy of Sears-Peyton Gallery: Shawn Dulaney, MaryBeth Thielhelm, and Cecil Touchon.

Catering on location
Food & Company, Edie Goettler (Edie's Catering), The Golden Pear Café, Kass Kapsiak (Catering by Kass), Chris Ludwick (Grape Vine Catering Company), Jesse A. Rivas, and Spoon Catering

Providing assistance, advice, or support
Allison Arieff, Jim Baldwin, Emma Boys, Monica Bhargava, Garrett Burdick, Joe Byrnes, Greg Cann, Noël Casiano, Val Cipollone, Anne Crary, Marti Emmons, Christie Every, Holly Harrison, Catherine Hill, Sam Hoffman (New Lab), Anjana Kacker, Katherine L. Kaiser, Bob Kapoor (Duggal Color Projects), Maneli Keshavarzi, Steve Knowlden, Susan Kokot-Stokes, Randall Koll, Holly Li, Charlene Lowe, Andrew Mann, Jennifer Martin, Frank Millero, Dung Ngo, Emily Noh, Joan Olson, Pottery Barn Creative Services, Patrick Printy, Andrea Raisfeld, Philip Rosseti, Cynthia Rubin, Diana Schrage Peter Scott, Karen Shapiro, Amy Shebes, Anthony Spurlock, Jason Stewart, Esther Tamondong, Sara Terrien, Scot Velardo, Juli Vendzules, The Village Latch Inn, Colin Wheatland, and Dena Zemsky

All photography by Hotze Eisma, except for:
Jacket front flap, photography by Christina Schmidhofer © 2003. Materials swatches in Design Details and Find Your Style, photography by Dan Clark. Pages 118, 180 (bottom right), 181 (bottom right), photography by Alan Williams.

About Pottery Barn

Founded in 1949 as a single store in Manhattan, Pottery Barn has evolved into America's leading source for style. For more than fifty years, Pottery Barn has brought comfort, style, and inspiration to people who love their homes. You can shop from Pottery Barn by calling 1-800-922-5507, by visiting us online at www.potterybarn.com, or by stopping by a store near you.